These Words Work.

Comments on Love, Learning, and Life., Volume 1

Cornelious "See" Flowers

Published by See the Poet LLC, 2024.

THESE WORDS WORK.
Comments on Love, Learning, and Life.
VOLUME ONE

Cornelious "See" Flowers

See the Poet LLC
P.O.Box
Country Club Hills, IL
312.515.8572

These Words Work. Vol. 1

©2024 Cornelious "See" Flowers

All rights reserved, including the right to reproduce this book or portions thereof in any form whatsoever. For information and permissions, inquiries may be addressed to See the Poet LLC.

Any attempt made to copy, steal, or take credit for the material in this book without the expressed written permission and approval of the author will be pursued and prosecuted according to the copyright laws and guidelines in the applicable jurisdiction.

For bulk purchases and discounts for educational purposes, contact the author via email at booking@seethepoet.com.

Cornelious "See" Flowers
Facebook: Cornelious Flowers
Instagram: @seethepoet
X: @seethepoet
YouTube: @seethepoet
Website: www.seethepoet,com

Table of Contents

And then	1
Love	5
How...	7
LOVE SONG	10
To My Son	12
Word, silly little word.	14
The bus stop, LOVE.	16
Different	18
I wish...	19
Games, of love (Mind)	21
Impulse	22
Streets	23
Untrue.	24
Where is hope.	26
Of course... (A Parent's Love)	28
Dreaming.	30
Shouldn't have...	31
It's raining... Come...	32
I wish...	33
Next Lifetime	34
God is... (The gist)	36
Gone Crying.	37
Reminder (Songs)	39
Awaken (Alive)	41
My Poetry	45
Let you go.	46
For the Old Man	48
Battle, lines.	50
In a way.	51
Talk to Me.	52
Shadows...	54

In our own image. 55
In relationship... (In relation to) 56
Reveal. 57
Spirit Full. 58
Shine. 59
Red Line (Blurred) 61
Since then. 63
My Prayer for Success... 64
Grace, Amazing. 65
Open... 66
Belief... (Remembering) 68
Proceed, naked. 69
Sad Love Poem (About You) 70
Forgive Yourself. 73
Know-It-All. 79
Multiplicity. 83
Ignorant. 86
On top. 88
Eventually. 89
The give. 90
Dreaming dream 91
Outside within 92
Alcoholic 95
Mistakes 96
Fix 98
Prayer for Success. 101
The truth. 103
Hidden. 104
Intent. 106
Served. 108
Fall. 112
Lovesense. 113
Action 114

Her idea	115
Perceived threat	118
Posts	119
Double entendre	122
Our clothes	125
More to it	128
What is real	130
Scars	133
Independent	134
I want you	136
Failure is not an option.	139
Fire (For You)	144
Work in Progress	146
Always love	148
Love Me	149
Model	152
Hustle	155
Sweet tooth	157
You love me	158
This me... (No one knows)	160
Love, finally.	164
My wish for you...	166
Rescued... (for Love)	168
Regrets... (of Love)	170
Don't be so hard on YOU.	171
Abandoned, reckless.	173
Relentlessly	174
Speak my mind	177
Decidedly	180
Write for You	182
It Blows... (Death)	185
Our Father, or not	186
Self-Imploded	190

What's next... (After I'm so...) 193
Mission "Aborted" 196
I like you, plain. 199
Don't Shoot. 203
Name calling 207
She fell in love, with words. 212
What if. 214
God-less 218

INTRODUCTION

There are enough words in these poems.
No need for an introduction.
Enjoy.

And then...

And then
there will be something else
something more
something harder
different
more requiring
more challenging
expensive
unexpected
that hurts
and then you will have to go
and keep going
because there is no other way
to make sense of it
or to stop it
and then
the distractions
the delays
the doubts
the distance
the decisions
that you must consider
and then
the devil
that you blame
responsible
that keeps trying to stop you
from stopping him
because you could
stop him

if you wanted to
because you're bigger
because faith is bigger
than whatever is not faith
even the biggest thing
is smaller than the smallest faith
and you tell yourself that
and then
someone says you're crazy
because you believe
when they say you shouldn't
because they couldn't
because somebody told them
that they wouldn't
and then
they take a seat
to watch you
fall
harder
faster
and then you do
fall
harder
faster
right onto your purpose
your destiny
on purpose
somehow
and someone is watching you
for an example
and you don't see them
because

THESE WORDS WORK.

all you see is in front of you
and you try to focus
on that
and then
more of
the distractions
the delays
the doubts
the distance
the decisions
that you must consider more
in order to keep fighting
in order to keep living
because living is your fight
living is why you fight
so you ready for war
and then
someone smiles
someone special
someone who doesn't see
the war
only that you're fighting
and they ask why
and you don't know what to say
so you smile back
holding back tears
and the pain
and the frustration
and the problems
because you don't want them
to see the worse that is to come
because you want them

to have a bigger faith
a better faith
and then
you realize that
there is no different faith
just faith
and so you smile back
to reassure them
that help is on the way
in spite of
the distractions
the delays
the doubts
the distance
the decisions
that they must consider
while they fight
while they live
and then
it happens again
because it always happens again
whether you're ready or not
because it doesn't need you
to be ready
it just needs you
to be.

Love

Sometimes the one you love
is not the one you love
but instead the one you want
and they know that
but they want to be wanted
and so they allow you to love them
because they need you to validate
that they matter
because you need them to validate
that you have feelings
or that you tried to
or that you cared
or that you tried to
or that you showed up
or that you tried to
when no one else would
or when the one they wanted to
didn't
and that is just love
doesn't make much sense
but it makes people happy
or makes them want to be happy
and gives them this feeling
that some people think is happiness
even though it hurts
even though it forces you to give up
fighting
for the right thing
because the wrong thing makes sense
love makes the wrong things make sense

because love makes sense of everything
especially the things that don't
so you do the stupid
dumb
reckless
careless
selfish
selfless
selflessly selfish
stupid selflessly selfish
things
because of love
because it feels right
even when you know it's not
LOVE
and sometimes the one you love
is not the one you love
just the one who makes you feel good
or bad enough to make you feel
something like you're wanted
something like this.

How...

Heartbreak is the only reason to keep on loving
Or trying to find love where there is no pain....
Or finding patience in pain because pain attracts healing and cures
And forgiveness becomes a reason to be hurt again or an excuse you can use to justify why you do any of it...
Sex is how you explain it
Because words can't and no one seems to speak your language when it comes to things that matter
And since sex seems to matter you make it a matter-of-factly type of means of communicating when you can't
And it seems that you never do
But you keep trying...
Trying to make love to make sense to make something better because the thought makes you feel good
Or a memory makes you feel good
Or a fantasy makes you imagine that it will feel good
And maybe it does, if it does, when it does
But it does absolutely nothing to change anything significant
Because sex is definitely not significant
When it comes to love
It just magnifies heartbreak
And makes things difficult
And different
And makes fools of people who think that they are smarter than love
Or heartbreak
Or pain
Or anything that requires you to surrender possibility to the probability
That you will inevitably feel absolutely nothing as it overtakes you

Blame it on the chemical avalanche that rushes you and depletes you of rationality...
Yes, it's a mess
Trying to fix broken people with broken means, things you picked up from other broken people,
Who are just being
The truth is that you only want to when you have no choice but to and that will only make things seem more important than what they really are until you realize that the only things that matter are the things that don't mean enough to distract you from what gives you a chance to love
Without questions
Or sufficient answers
Or expectations
That judge mistakes
And circumvent adventure
With the chance to wait
Your soul doesn't care what happened nor what is next
It cries out to give its best
To illuminate from behind the desk
That contains all of the files you've amassed and collected and repeatedly over-checked for where you could have done different
And maybe some type of map that could lead you from this prison
That holds you hostage and forces you to listen
To the sound of echoes that beckons you from assumption
Your memory only knows where it once was
Not where you're going to be,
Heartbreak is the only thing that will make you able to see,
Just how foolish it all had came to be
Until you care enough to remain at ease
And breathe
The real sigh of relief

THESE WORDS WORK.

That makes you free.

LOVE SONG

You fit the lyrics to every love song
All too well
John Mayer to Lenny Williams
Dru to Lauryn Hill
And I don't understand you still
You make since when I need convincing
but not when my curiosity begins itching
and you start bitching
about how I don't match the me you see
But you refuse to let me leave
Or let me see what it's like without you
And so I have to doubt you
Maybe it is the pain that I've brought you
Sigh
That's what happens when it really doesn't
When a true love defines a soul mate that wasn't
And it doesn't feel good
Sigh
Before I ask why
Musiq and Maxwell don't make it no better
Just as confusing as reading old love letters
I've gone all the way from Dave Hollister to Nickelback,
But no song can fix that...
And there's this song that I keep hearing
Fearing every next word that comes because every last word sounds
like this
Feels like a punch, feels like a kiss
One of those songs you look forward to, but you miss
Cry

THESE WORDS WORK.

Trying to hold back from saying that this feels like we're delaying the inevitable,
Betting on the results of horoscopes and the odds of anecdotes that stem from poems I wrote that had nothing to do with you
Brought into question whether or not my words were true or if my motives were used for ulterior gain,
But why should I change?
And all the while this song plays
The song says:
Love is what happens after everything goes wrong and all that is left are words without song, things that seem permanent seem better off gone and assumptions appear short but rather stay long,
Trust becomes trust when someone's betrayed and forgiveness only exist because pain finds its way,
Consistency doesn't matter if surprise makes such meaningless,
Nor does giving have value if you take so much shit,
Cry
And this song keeps on playing,
Louder per note
And then I recognize it,
The last song that I wrote.

To My Son...

So many things I will teach you
while hoping that the walls of my waters don't ever breach you
And if I were to break,
that my stains should never reach you
In you I see where I began
I hope that you see in me reflection of a man
With that information,
I want you to STAND
Believe in good despite any urges or suggestion different
Where there is an option for your voice or your ear,
Listen
Position yourself to be able to try
There is no reason for you to suffer,
there is no reason FOR YOU to lie
Love because you have no reason not to
Feel because you have a feeling that you've got to
Share because you never want to be without
and Travel, so that you know what life is about
Remember that people are people
and that is no excuse
But instead a reason to forgive
or whichsoever you choose
How I've done it was my way
and I will never hide those facts
But Son learn from any if my mistakes
and to the same you will never go back
Show the world that you need them
but that on some can not you compromise
So that YOU LEAVE FOR YOUR SON
ACTIONS FOR WHICH YOU WON'T APOLOGIZE

THESE WORDS WORK.

And above all know that YOU are loved
and how much you mean,
For if everything that matters is right on the inside,
then of YOU, to the world it will be seen.
Love,
Dad.

Word, silly little word.

There was once a word I knew
then we became friends
the word and I grew close
almost seemed like pretend
Me and the word shared feeling
hid snug in one another's embrace
the word and I sought pleasure
a thing we both desired to taste
The word had a little history
and I begged to learn the story
but the word found me more interesting
thought I'd find its life somewhat boring
I screamed at the word to help me
just not to assume and let us be
but the word had known another
and saw glimpses of such in me
Another had used word wrong
one had only used word to call
some had used word differently
few had even used word at all
Now word knew me as an adjective
though adverbs are more preferred
then word gave me an ultimatum
a bigger word albeit absurd
Word said that I should be silent
Word said that I couldn't see
Word said that I should be better
I guess something other than me
And now my lips are silent
for words word I no longer hear

THESE WORDS WORK.

word had the audacity to question
an answer made perfectly clear
Now word is just a fantasy
an imaginary little boys dream
some other idiots objective
some silly ole pessimists plea
Word means nothing to a doer
But doing is not what word sees
word awaits a very long paragraph,
a sentence is all that we need.

The bus stop, LOVE.

At the bus stop of love
On the corner of here and there
Just waiting on my ride
In this city named everywhere
I've missed a few on purpose
I've been late a few times
Guess I just enjoyed the people watching
Or I was trying to avoid the lines
You see it all from where I'm standing
You hear it all just the same
After all, they're just people
Somewhere in a midst of change
Today I have no destination
Just came alone for the ride
I might not meet somebody
Who am I kidding, there are seats to sit beside
So today i'll meet a stranger
A girl who looks like fun
I'll pick the one without the bags
Just in case we need to run
Tomorrow I'll meet another
I may fancy something plain
A girl who looks like mother
Maybe sounding just the same
And next week I'll find a lover
One who wears such on her sleeve
And I will tell her about my search for love
Until in destiny she believes
Next month, next year, no differences
These routes remain the source

THESE WORDS WORK.

As long as I stand at this bus stop,
Only love will be the course
Or somedays I walk
Maybe find a park to rest
Other days I'll stay at home
Seems like there I'm at my best
Find courage to ticket a plane
Soon I will try to brave the sea
I think I like climbing mountains
If I don't I soon will see
But yet I'm still just at this bus stop
And it all just seems so plain
I'm tired of what I see here
Tomorrow I'll take the train.

Different

The darkness hides my tears well
and so I dwell inside of myself
cloaked inside of my own failure
in spite of myself
Feelings left to bare the loneliness
of being only just an only self
leaving me to breathe silently
but only help
Wondering if I could ever be
maybe something else
a someone who had known better
or just...

I wish...

I wish that my brothers would dream and come alive in hope
while witnessing the come to pass of every plan he's wrote,
I wish that my sisters would believe and rest assured in trust
while experiencing the point of it all that explains the meaning of
enough,
I wish that my sons would grow and find every chance in life
while becoming men that afford such to their children and thus living
existing in right,
I wish that my daughters would be found while losing sense of having
to be
and instead identifying in self and establishing peace while exuding
belief,
I wish that my friends would be authentic and stand firm in who they
are
while challenging me to the better as our differences fall apart,
I wish that my teachers would be examples and give me credible
reasons to pursue
while offering a curriculum of my best interest and giving me
leadership as its due,
I wish that my pastors would be flawed and hold themselves to a
standard of me
while congregating the word with their walk so that in a sinner a
sinner can believe,
I wish that my family would be family and as a family come together
in sync
while as a family covering stable our bloodline as a family and not just
surrendering to defeat,
I wish that my leaders would be followers and think like humans
towards solution

while ignoring urges to be monsters neglecting the effects of material pollution,
I wish that I could just have wishes and not choices that lead me to see that while I can want as I want for forever, the only thing I can want for the better is me...

Games, of love (Mind)

I told you every lie you needed to hear in order for me to disappear,
I hid behind every time you closed your eyes hoping that a "maybe next time" would reappear,
I gave you hope that time would prove that time had found you gone,
that what you had was not in fact but instead just something wrong,
I showed you love in deferent to sides so that you'd let love be,
but gave you reason right to hate him so and wrong to not love me,
I threw away your gifts of care instead I hoarded fear,
in stress I found your soul existent rumbled over near,
In darkness kept your smiles and laughs so that you'd cry them out,
while toying with the pickled soul you've offered me to spout,
I gave you joys of pain and turned them to and fro,
escaping gaping holes of fear without a way to go,
Covered dreams in tastes of suit with candied coated shells,
But pit them on a plane to space and sunk them into wells
Fasted cries so slow that peace was nowhere near to find,
And yet I taught you nothing more than games within your mind...

Impulse

Moments are meant for times like this,
When eyes remiss over blind eyed bliss,
When things we shouldn't do find a time to enlist
every idea that accompanies our kiss,
Our bodies touch to agree that we might,
While our minds argue that our spirits are right,
Our fingers find crevices once impossible to excite
as our tongues tie knots in our imaginations light,
Excuses find reasons to escape in the dark,
We justify passion by pacing in parts,
Our scents intoxicate chased by the spark
Of a time such as this,
a safe place to start,
Pull me inside,
I've dreamed of such joy,
I'm warm and I'm willing,
A seamless enjoy,
I come with no carry,
I've eased into coy,
Just give me your heavy,
as things I employ,
Tonight is our given,
A moment of such,
This is no prison,
I'm free to be touch,
Just bring me unleavened,
and seize me at once
I won't be forgiven,
If sudden I must...

Streets

And no none was there when it happened
but the evil that circumstance captured
and all that could say to the statue
was too soon a memory left captioned
Their guns are no match for their lack
and so easily hunger they pack
they watch from their terrace of terror
for a victim to unknowingly snatch
A vitriol feeling towards merry
does instead give its way into fear
but as none can attest,
they are robbed of the nest,
and this violence is the lullaby cheer
They song and chant dance in the moment
as grass burns high to their treat
they swallow of potion forth yawning
while poisons and perish they eat
Who cry now reasons to save them
no prisoner calls back to be slain
for this a trap of such choosing
and nothing want more of the same
Their leather and trappings forewarned,
their leaders give reason to break
for this is their season to choice
and winter so soon is no make
But babies left standing in spring
are the spoils to a summer to come
the horns cry out to the coming,
run baby, run baby,
yes run.

Untrue.

It is never as it seems
or so suggest that I should find
while a love I'd hoped to possess
was not just a love of mine
Things happen, humans feel
trust must be given at the least
what takes place behind my back,
surely breaks in front of me
Secret kisses, purposed touch
I've feared it all the same
wanting wonder in its darkness
that whose you are would call my name
Or that you'd not give him my body
as said was mine yours whole to be
yet at any given moment
you've shared with them what's gone to me
Stupid promises and hopes,
just outright selfish lies,
You could have had me as an option,
Why'd you make me compromise
I know not that he knows just as much
my smile is placed to let him know
how dare you keep him warm inside
You told me you let him go
That taste so sour unfamiliar,
that recognized me pause
You've let him wash away my paint
with his stains aside your walls
And it is jest he finds to introduce
when path of ours doth meet

THESE WORDS WORK.

He gets to hide behind the truth
I'm exposed behind defeat
And titles given that I've known
made not much sense before
You rest assured that all was pure
when I knew that there was more
And so many played this game as well
as if the joke was I
an orchestrated scheme of sorts
to keep me standing by
So tears should crash and years should pass,
you'd still be lying near
How could you live inside yourself
knowing true what's been so clear
That you never wanted just as me
just "you and I" was not
Instead you gave your all to all
and left me with what I got
I've prayed and sought counsel,
cried and changed
unsuspectingly sharing my hurt
When all along unbeknownst to me,
you never had intentions to work
A laughing stock,
the towns great fool,
a victim of love once was,
So yet don't wonder,
nor threat nor thunder
You deserve my absence,
Because.

Where is hope...

What happened to hope,
was it murdered just as was she
an innocent baby just died,
it appears hope also left the scene
And what's to be said of good,
there must've been good somewhere
can't be that all witnesses were bad
and that bad was the only one fair
Surely someone else cares
certainly care gave a shit,
or does no one really give a fuck
and our life is but what we make of it
No conscious, remorse or pause,
one of these bandits did feel,
but neither concern or urge would cause
a selfish evil to reveal
And naught a samaritans job
to be willing to open their mouth
for its but a video game to play
And a restart to let them out
So what became of cause?
The reason that deed was done,
Can we really blame being irresponsible on the ignorant senses of guns
And poor and lost and embarrassed
Surely they share in this rage,
Because they are just as much to blame
As every rapper that takes his stage
The poets, the parents, the pimps
have access as easy as any
And they, the biggest of lies,

THESE WORDS WORK.

for opinions they share with us many
Well what happened to Faith,
I know faith, Faith wouldn't deceive
Or is faith just open on Sundays?
for a price you wouldn't believe...
The truth? The truth won't ignore,
The truth has facts to dispense
But the truth is just another murder,
and the truth is no evidence.

Of course... (A Parent's Love)

And the child said to the parent
Will I ever have a chance?
And the parent so responded
With every hope I pray you can.
And the parent did continue
I will give all that I have.
And the child assured responded
Then these questions must I ask.
Could you give me every secret
that I may know your truth
and with it give me understanding
that I may know its use...
Shall you lead me with examples
show me ways through exercise,
Can you expose me to your faults
that I might know your cries...
Will you explain as you have erred
without pride expose your be,
Can you instead of hiding life
open up its doors for me..
And since surely I will fail you
in time of certain youth,
Can you treat me as you once were
giving testimony as proof...
And the parent so prepared,
knowing sure this day would come
gave quickly these responses
of his heart where it was from...
My child I've known your questions
and the answers I have searched,

THESE WORDS WORK.

Most of them were surely pondered
long before your birth...
As it hurt to have any secret,
and it's darkness that such held,
I've made promise to release you
from any prison of my dwell
And so exposed are there my action
living proof of what to come,
and rest assured that I have weakness,
many tears have made me strong...
I have done and I have seen,
a road thus traveled had its be,
but I give to you my life exposed,
may be whatever, but it was me...
And there is nothing you can do
that can ever take away,
the joy that fills me from being your parent,
and such enjoying every day...

Dreaming

Dreams
Of the reachable
lessons teachable through example
vision keen enough to handle
obstacles that surely come
Dreams
Beyond every imagination
and constellation
and sky that holds the promise
that we suggest possible
Dreams
That give way to fight
unlike any fight that had before
and with it strength that endures
bringing with it more
Dreams
Of all that is happily
and coming after what we've hoped
chasing down our ambitions
proving bigger what we've spoke
Dreams
In the midst of trial and talent
lying balance at our nose
so that we may sense coming true
of what our purpose doth propose
Dreams

Shouldn't have...

I take the chance every time that I meet somebody different
that I will be reminded of you and feel the need to rekindle
or at least consider that nothing was wrong and in fact just something missing
and then it gets me,
So I call to see how you are and surprisingly it'll be me that just the other day you mentioned
and you were reflecting on my pension for giving you some sort of feeling
and of course I begin to remember,
And before we know better we decide that maybe we should have never ceased to be
because in the middle of it all we had great moments and times shared
and you're still important to me
plus the fact that I still remember how good you made me feel intimately
never mind the ups and downs of my spirit, the ins and outs of my psyche, or what I went through mentally,
And we are there again, familiar and comfortable and excited
both of us just as intoxicated as the other, ignited
no better understood than before, just lightened
for this time we carry no expectations, just heightened
And it feels good, at first, or just at that time
long enough for me to remember how you won't forget that time
and as quickly as it restarted it'll end because of that time
for the truth is that anything that we were, had died, at that time

It's raining... Come...

Come stand in the rain with me
close your eyes and make a wish
Make a smile that says you want it
and I will make it this
Come walk in the rain with me
not far but out of sight
Let's find a place to enjoy it
Undisturbed throughout the night
Come play in the rain with me
Let us touch and fall apart
And at the same time come together
soaking wet while in the dark
Come run in the rain with me
let precipitation be our sweat
Let me chase until I catch you
Let me catch you while you're wet
Come dance in the rain with me
any move your heart desires
Teach me something from your songbook
to the sound these drops supply us
Come enjoy this lovely rain with me
and we could do it all
Maybe we could make a puddle
as the rain we make will fall...
Come, it's raining...

I wish...

I wish I knew the words,
to the song that sets you free
to the story that releases your heart
to the poem that allows you to breathe
I know I have the courage,
to sing that song to you
where my voice can't meet the notes
my lyrics and truth will do
I believe I have the power,
to give you all you seek
to collapse any barrier before you
to build what will become we
I imagine I have the passion
to write the story with heart
and give depth to every layer
and purpose to every part
I hope I have the time,
to give you all those things
to make every word of it action
to have us come to be
I surely have the talent
to write that poem and recite it
on a stage that you've selected
at a time that you've decided
Because,
I feel I have a reason
to want you in my life
though I might not have it all,
I have the things that make it right.

Next Lifetime

I thank you
for making me wait long enough to realize that you're not worth it
and nobody's perfect
but you've made me realize that I'm so much more than settling for
you that it's almost hilarious to me remembering where I was headed
towards when I wasn't thinking
but I wasn't thinking
I was doing, something that I shouldn't have albeit action none the
less and to suggest that I didn't know any better is to question more
than just my intentions but my intellect and it actually brings to
mention my integrity and letting me get by on just that I was naive
would be like comparing tattoos to scars
Now who wants a sleeve?
you wouldn't believe that I actually wanted to create of you what I
didn't get from you by giving you what is in me for free,
yes you would,
in fact you believed
You thought that I was so intrigued that I would indeed let you be
while I became and for your nothingness you'd be rewarded fame and
the same energy that I expended to give you matter would be what I
held onto after you certainly decided to give someone else what I had
required of you for some time
some time
to consider that you were not just selfish but in addition to helpless a
malfeasance of sorts because you had been elected by me to what
would have been a lifetime appointment but you didn't even have time
for the moment, just lies and disappointment
Salutations
These words are me waving bye like ole girl from Color Purple
thinking that any and every wish that you have ill towards me will only

hurt you because I don't even see you now, I've worked through the emotions and feeling like I need to stay because at one time I did say that I'd never give up on you...
well that was meant for the who that I thought you were, the who that you pretended to be, the who that I imagined was the who for me, the who that brought the parts and pieces that I needed to assemble greatness, don't worry about the time, it was you I wasted, you I chased with reckless abandon, you that stranded every option and opportunity by choosing me to handle so loosely, I offered you entry into my spiral when you were just loose-leaf, a sheet in a desperate wind, tending towards a "less than" end and the stupid part is that you are who you were when we began
A friend.

God is... (The gist)

God is
everything that happens
beginning to end
and in between
the good and the bad
even the mean
if so you believe
if not
then
God is
pretend
and nothing to do with faith
or men
just a coincidence
and a quote
that gives it sense
and a reckless confidence
that is on the fence
about sin
or why we exist.

Gone Crying

I want you to cry every time
I say I love you
because you know me
and how hard it was for me to open
my heart
to anyone
because of everyone
that broke it
but you awoke it
spoke it back to life with life
made me write
which made me right
which made me try
which gave me life
and that
makes you cry
so much so that it seems like pain
and makes me realize
that it looks the same
just like the chance
to understand
looks like romance
and what looks like a struggle
from afar
looks like a dance
in your eyes
and so I cry
now you know why
I'm not always looking
when you mention me

not paying attention
but relieved
that we sometimes see
eye to eye
or that you always seem to find
something in mine
that makes it right
to keep in mind
that I've come so far
from so far behind
and standing here now
gives me great pleasure
to decide
to keep on trying
to remind myself
that you are nothing like
anyone else
and yet you still love me
despite
my night
that separates your day
from so many ways
that could have made you leaving
much easier
even if
I stopped breathing
the moment you left
so I'm just here
crying
all by myself

Reminder (Songs)

How do you miss what isn't gone
or try to make right what isn't wrong
Trying to do both while listening to songs
that remind you of them
Conjuring up a feeling
that isn't gone
finding lights dim
sparking bright memories
of silly things
that start silly dreams
that survive outside the dark
wishing they would
have a reason to argue
something to spark
the value of that conversation that usually happens
after things went different
like they always did
when you mentioned more
now it's less
and you want to suggest that you'd be willing
to listening more
whatever it takes
to get you in a positioning force
that might
give you the right to say
goodbye the right way
where gone is just a nights stay
and home is where
the two of you
begin the lights day

and one of you
just might say
Something that makes now
seem like
it never happened
that is
if it ever happens
But,
How do you miss what isn't gone
or try to make right what isn't wrong
Trying to do both while listening to songs
that remind you of them
On repeat again
And somehow
seeming to be selected
in order
in order to leave you
rejecting
the borders
testing the boundaries of casual and no attachments
just to see
if something happens
like acting
Scenes from
the predetermined scripts
that slipped your mind
out of your mouth
hopefully into the ears
Of the one
that the song
on the radio
is about.

Awaken (Alive)

I wonder if anyone notices
that I walked away
left
everything they said was right
for me
so that I'd sooner be
worthy
gave up my sanity
so that I may be ready
for the craziness
that came for me
when I spoke death
to the things that damaged me
they only see that I was gone
guessed and hypothesized
quite often criticized
as to my why's
without ever asking me
suggestion that I took leave
was why I couldn't breathe
choking on the smoke
of their trees
burned fruit only makes jam
to be put in a can
and that Sir,
that wasn't me
labeled "all natural"
preservatives added
artificial flavors
and even coloring

readily available on aisle 3
next to the pornography
and the gambling
and the mediocrity
packages of hope and faith
tucked somewhere in between
they brought it
I brought into it
stupid investment
a return of "been through it"
now I know to check it out
then do it
salvation available
for good sayings,
and a powerful poem
some profound verbiage
and they all goin'
don't know nothin'
'bout the All Knowing
or what I really look like
without the robe
they were satisfied talking
about the clothes
which don't fit the occasion
let alone the man
but what garment is appropriate
when you're chosen to stand
loose fitting true religion
or another brand
of even tighter pants
I think she noticed me
recognizing my wife in her

THESE WORDS WORK.

but she can't handle my truth
let alone my life in her
so I'll just be whatever she says
something on the side
another knife in hers
I wish she would have though
because I could have been had more
but no reason to
just brings him them bad lore
and I could deal with it
but what for
then I see her again last night
and I wanted to make things right
but of course she just left early
couldn't see past sight
would've chased her but
that would have wasted what
I been working 3 years
to face her
once
I gave up everything
forgot almost everything
and almost remembered my past
'till a voice reminded me
that I can comeback
and this time I'll be
better
capital letters
longer sentences
clear thoughts possible
through repentance's
and great

maybe just a little bit late
but I can't fall asleep anymore
a new generation to awake
for sake
my son's and mine
both in the same boat
Alive.

My Poetry

I find it ridiculous that one should edit or correct poetry which in itself is perfect because of its incorrectness and should not be subject to the established ideas and rules of a much maligned society that guards heavy the reliance on an educational system so egregiously opposite to the pureness of the heart that creates these atmospheres of words. There is no mutual agreement in the wars of such words for they are intended to represent feeling and feeling can not be corrected it can only be changed and by that it is a different thing altogether. I offer that you write your poetry and rest it assured in the confidence of your intentions or insecurities or inspirations or inhibitions. It is yours, yours to leave as stupid or surreal, as serious or serendipitous. Poetry is the explanation to our most awesome of questions and the answer to our most specific of query. It makes its sense on the backs of the illogical, the erratic, the loose-fitting, off-balanced, awkward, ridiculous, repulsive, dark, sensitive, and authentic reality. Poetry is the bystanders account intended to relay, for those who desire, a message of opinion powered to transcend the uniform, overcome the authoritative, strengthen the weak, empower the hopeless, discover the lost, or comfort the broken. Poetry, in its beauty, justifies the scars and hurts of scores that seek out its shelter in the darkest of hours, relaxing fears and doubts alike in the obliging arms of the humorous, colorful, sultry, truthful narratives of strangers or established pens that release with no rule or control but those self-imposed to protect the sanity of bringing forth what falls from the recesses of their individual capacities. Yes, poetry is the excuse and the exception, both to the rule and yet to the justification of its disregard. So no, you may not "correct" my poetry. You may interpret it as you shall, you can deem it as it delivers to you but it is mine, as I wrote it, and I won't change it.

-see

Let you go.

I want to hear about and see you free,
I want to witness you experience new things,
I want to see you breathe,
leaving everything that chokes you behind and going forward to find...
an air that coats you in the new of how and thus coaxes you to plow
head first into the distinct possibilities of now...
I want you to leave,
run away from the former things and maybe just for a second
remember me,
right before you breathe,
right before you see things differently,
I want you to close your eyes
and be able to see,
so that you realize that nothing about who we are is typically,
but keeping your eyes closed
I want you to jump,
from memory,
and land in the spot that has long avoided your desires,
mentally,
and before you open them
I want you to reach,
spiritually,
and feel the strength of my words, lyrically...
Then I want you to breathe, literally,
say with your existence
those things you once resisted,
and know that I may not speak of the spot you left in my life, but I've
kissed it,
frequently,
hoping to cover the fact

THESE WORDS WORK.

that I wanted you to go,
and I didn't see it all the time,
but I've witnessed it,
I needed you to show me how close we were,
through distances...
And now I get it,
fresh air,
well instances,
for instance, that's what this is.

For the Old Man

For the old man...
I'm crying
for the old man
that as a young man
never managed
and now as an old man
is only damaged
no longer a whole man
so he's stranded
left to fend for leftovers
from the last place he slept over
so he's famished
no complexion
just blemished
no facade
its vanished
wishing history would repeat
so he can replenish
or he's finished
So for the old man I plan it
so that I don't panic
in him I see incomplete
no image
no advantage
he can't sit down
from no standards
didn't heed warnings
now he's empty handed
by definition a bastard
by default a bandit

THESE WORDS WORK.

his excuses routine
his existence random
should've, would've, could've
his anthem...
So I'm crying
for the old man
that as a young man
never managed
and now as an old man
is only damaged
no longer a whole man
so he's stranded...

Battle, lines...

The time we spend
arguing
is borrowing away from us
bargaining
sending our further
farther away from us
arduous
how we approach the argument
adamant
that neither started it
but hardened
making it harder than it already is
but so far away
from where it started
and the funny part then,
is...
We fight for no reason
just as hard
as we do for reasons
beyond that either of us can explain
until the evens make odds
and leave us with scars
equal to our pain
but seemingly for applause
to the cheers of our crowded minds
fighting
to break down the walls
that are hiding
our flaws

In a way...

She got away
because she got a way
of being
and I got in her way
not seeing things
the same way
being
too comfortable with things
being the same way
thinking
when I should have just said it
that I liked what she did
anyway
any way
but I just said okay
and that was never enough
and I can see why
she could leave it
the same way
she found it
but different
the same thing
a same thing
everyday
is just what she said,
crazy
in a way.

Talk to Me.

I want to talk to you
but not on the phone
and not with words
but with feeling
so that it means something
and leaves nothing out
us,
that's what I want to talk about
and everything that has changed
since we've been separate ways,
the day before yesterday
just hasn't been the same
nothing to do but change
I want your thoughts about it
but we don't have to talk about it
just make sound with our body parts
then put our mouths around it
I want to talk to you
hear your story in a different way
find that your skin has an opinion
more than your lips could say
but I'll hear them too
when I'm near you
move
to the sound of conversation
that we make with our legs
apologizing with our hands
as our eyes begin to beg
I really want to talk to you
in a foreign language

THESE WORDS WORK.

maybe two or three
in a universal tongue,
created by you and me
and come up with a song
that our feet can sing
as we dance with our breath,
repeatedly...
Please talk to me
I want to talk to you
about differences
and about talking to much
without listening
without mentioning our past
or who we talked to last
if you don't want to know,
I promise not to ask,
But you have to talk to me.

Shadows...

It is in the shadow of our past that we learn to experience the pain as a journey. What we have gone through was necessary to produce the now that explains what we lost, why we left, how we learned, who we loved, where we've been, and when it was time to move on. In those shadows are our purposes, are our platforms, in those dark places are our podiums, are our peace. There, behind us, is where we discovered our strengths and decided our ability to fight for reasons or even the excuses that we found refuge in to hide us from uncomfortable or unfamiliar destiny or fates. We created those shadows by where we stood or sat, where we positioned ourselves, by virtue of where we chose to stand. We have carried those shadows and filled spaces with them. They have become our ghost, they hang on and haunt us to no end at even the hint of any light that finds its way towards our day. They have become our definition by meaning us well beyond our nows. They are of course, shadows. And those shadows create the shade that cover those that come behind us from the burning sun of exercise and experience unnecessary. It is in the shadows of our troubles that innocence may rest in the education of history. There, in the midst of our mistakes, our shadows, while they are gullible and naive, youth and immaturity may be guided and guarded for the good of protection against the shadows that are to come. They will learn in that dark to recognize what is and what is in light. They will become the stronger that we were only ambitious of, the wiser that we curiously suggested, and the courageous that our fears yearned to be. In the shadows. In our shadows.

-see

In our own image.

I dreamed
that GOD had dreams
like me and you
that came true,
me and you.

In relationship... (In relation to)

We've come to that point
and now we're pointing fingers
hoping to be free of the pain
but wanting the promise to linger
deciding to let nothing stop us
getting to where nothing brings us
somehow refusing to admit it,
that neither of us wants to be here.

Reveal.

So I may have
mistakingly
mistaken you
taken you for granted
by chasing you
staked my absence
on erasing you
confirmed my doubts
while facing you
made known my lies
by staying true.

Spirit Full...

Spirit will no longer ignore
what my situation is
Even as I pretend to "cope" with my "what is"
my soul cries out
to my emotions
and energy's
to expand...
To try, to push, to experiment, to experience
To give me a chance
So I'm up,
in the stillness of my reality, amidst the movement
of my awareness,
bittersweet with anxiety, restless but rested.
I am bound.
From both perspectives,
a two-sided evolution
of constant monotony
in the midst
of relentless change.
And then I close my eyes
to try to see clearly,
past the mediocrity,
imagining the possibility,
that opening my eyes
seems to steal from me, because
I just so happen to be
the only one,
that doesn't see,
the power,
in being me.

Shine

He once saw the sun as a dream
and he leaned in to realize himself
that dreams come true everyday
and lie every night
and come back in mornings
sometimes bright
sometimes amidst obstacles
and sometimes at different times
but they, dreams, are real
and the sun is proof
that dreams come true
and exist beyond limitations
or expectations
or beyond the reach of people
that can't see your dream
while its bright
but instead they recognize it only
in the dark of night
or in the shade of its shadows
unaligned with its flight
inconsiderate of its origin
or it's plight
even though they know a dream
is sufficient light
but they question it relentlessly
until he puts up a fight
to believe in his dream
and be burnt by it
to learn by it
so he stands student to the sun

empty class quiet
trying
to feel his dream
its warmth in such a cold place
eyes open, disrobed face
blemishes made and mended
by other dreams,
suns
that came and went
long before
and long after,
him
in seasons of lack and abundance
dreams are his thunders
his hailstorms and first fruits
his slim pickings and pursuits
his "on the horizon"
his "left behind"
his one reason to not press rewind
for neither he nor his fears
can stop him from dreaming
nor believing
in the sun.

Red Line (Blurred)

(Live poetry from my Red Line seat)
He clutches his purse
half smoked Newport in his fingers
that are polished purple
She's sees a friend in the crowd
"Hey Bitch" she yells
"Bitch I've been calling you" her friend eagerly retorts
The only language spoken on here
aloud
is foul
Real loud
Here comes some woman
running late
walking slow
fat, two kids in tow
one barefoot
she know
and now she's hitting him
for no reason
other than he didn't listen
to her instruction
where did he learn disruption
probably from this disfunction
and I think he's slow
she don't think,
she know
A circle
filled with "loose squares"
different prices
who cares

that I don't smoke
I got dreads
so I look like it
Real Blurred Lines

Since then...

I miss the feeling
of you next to me
gesturing
just as we
begin to play destiny
seeking to deeper our desires,
desperately
deciphering deities through dialogue,
coming together separately,
wrestling
testing the limits of our bodies,
sexually,
innocent actions,
done professionally
referencing experience,
through ecstasy
I miss your recipe
the way you make me feel,
especially
the way you serve me,
specifically
I miss that attention,
definitely
the times that you made it okay
by questioning
whether or not I was okay
with everything
supporting affectionately,
effectively
I miss making you smile,
my specialty,
and we did it naturally,
actually.

My Prayer for Success...

Dear Lord,
Guide my steps as I travel this road,
where all I desire walks with all I know
As I pursue my destiny and follow my dreams
I ask that You inspire my wants and allow for my needs
Could You show me favor that outweighs my faith
so that if I falter, You keep my pace
In my journey that will take me far and beyond,
I pray for Your constant protection
to keep me unharmed
I pray for wisdom, I pray for growth,
I pray for patience, which I need the most
I'd rather that You are my foundation before my family or friends
for I am rest assured You are there until the end
And in return, my Father, I give you my best
as I ask they You answer
My Prayer for Success,
Amen.

Grace, Amazing...

There is
something
about going through
the storm
prepared
that makes
a difference
when
the lightning
and the rain
and the wind
and hail
and the hell
comes
to destroy
everything
in its way,
There is something
about
being able to say,
"Thank You"
for
Amazing Grace.

Open...

There's a difference
between air-bending
and pretending
between being
and sending
the wrong message
pending interpretation
patience
ain't the same as waiting
for something to just happen
facing ain't the same
as dealing
and dying ain't the same
as being killed
so I'm filled with questions
suggestions to my integrity
because I let it be
didn't fight
when I was supposed to
shame and rejection
that I felt
prevented me
from exposing you
so I was exposed too
looked like the evil
that controlled you
and kept it all a secret
because I was told to
bended all the way
backwards

THESE WORDS WORK.

now you want me to fold too
NO
no chance
no deal
cancel Christmas
which is really what you did
cancelled Christmases
with your wickedness
and I've been getting the gift
re-gifted,
being a victim
wrapped and ripped
meticulously
believing that this
was all I could get
ridiculously
and more preposterous,
fictitiously
but now I know the difference
between you and me
and I get to release...
immediately.

Belief... (Remembering)

I remember remembering
my memories
of the many things
worth mentioning
from the beginning
the "anything's"
that you did for me
plenty of things
that had me considering
surrendering
sifting through
the significantly
and the itty bitty things
the so many things
that created this energy
that this reality is currently
giving me...
I'm learning to let go
of remembering
so that I can move on
from alone
to we...
belief.

Proceed, naked.

We write poetry
in nude poses
supposedly
in support of showing things
like how beautiful we are
as hopeless beings
as vocalist
in silent dreams
as token values
in broken schemes
as mad articulates
in spoken deeds
with our bodies
interwoven fiends
strewn across canvases
stolen by focused thieves
who rendezvous with dark
to expose their gleam
like innocent naked bodies
that disclose their needs
broken by disappointment
that bleeds
focused on old wisdom
that reads:
It's yours to give away,
proceed

Sad Love Poem (About You)

I find it funny
that you love me
that you care
that you're there
that you're aware
of me not loving you
the way you need me to
or need to be
but still believe
in the strangest things
like fairy tales
and make believe
and other things
that make me seem
worth the wait
or worth the chase
or worth the fate
that might be terrible
like only a taste
or a look at a menu
through a window
from a view
that has nothing
absolutely nothing
to do with you
but still you look
from where you are
reminding me with your pain
and showing me scars
that bear my name

THESE WORDS WORK.

your self-inflicted injury
inspired by me
and I find it funny
that you find me beautiful
after all the ugliness
that I put you through
and every other thing
that I made you lose
because you couldn't do both
love yourself and love me too
or take care of yourself
or responsibility
trying to prove to me
what it's like
when someone believes
but I didn't seem to notice
or even see
anything special
about how special you were
to me
instead it just seemed
that I laughed
at how you gasped
and choked
bended
and broke
you worried,
I wrote
you hurt,
I hoped
that you'd forget
and then relent

but instead I'd prepare
and you would pretend
that this would be
something different
something you could find funny
and far from true
like the sad love poems
that I write about you...

Forgive Yourself

Let them go,
vindicate your tears
with vision
remember that pain
with wisdom
listen
to the anxiety of haunting hopes
left dangling on the ropes
of regret
that mistake and maybe
left
incorrectly
cry those memories,
swiftly
then erase those thoughts
that linger,
quickly
because you need to release
so let it go
find peace intently,
intentionally,
but realistically
considering
that you are,
the most important thing,
the most vital entity,
the source of your energy
and anything
that restricts you
from being free

is an enemy
and if you allow,
they will supply in plenty,
unless
You let them go
forget to remember the hurt
if it helps you to move on
go by yourself,
if it is the only way
that you can go forward
or wait
until you recognize redemption
ignore the retention
or repetition
of repeating
cycles and seasons
that fertilize the reasons
that you can't grow beyond
the fences,
you planted
and then abandoned
something that you learned
as a lesson
from bad examples
let it go
breathing,
while holding your breathe,
for revenge,
is stupid
and impossible
a self-imposed obstacle,
optional,

THESE WORDS WORK.

and you are lucid,
a truth to be proven
so prove it,
by letting go
of hopeless and hindering,
of loneliness lingering,
or anything,
that is captivity,
and be free
go to a mirror
and see
look inside of your reflection
and recognize peace,
then release
imagine your hearts desire
then dream
seize the moment
as you speak,
BELIEF
BELIEVE,
that you can let it all go
know that life happens
because it has to
and that doesn't mean
that life is chasing after you
lose,
your grip on grief
and your idea
that you deserve mediocrity
because you messed up,
YOU ARE NOT PERFECT,
you just messed up

and that is going to happen,
it just does
to everyone,
INCLUDING YOU
so let it go
forgive yourself,
for not being there,
or being there too long,
for thinking you were right,
for being wrong,
for staying,
for being gone,
for lying,
for denying,
for taking,
for making the mistakes,
anyone,
whichever one,
all of them that you made,
in the first place,
for saying what you said,
or for saying nothing,
for doing "you",
when you could have done,
something
better
for letting years go by,
while silence festered,
and you never gestured
towards an apology
probably
because you were hurt

THESE WORDS WORK.

and you responded
or reacted
with a reaction
that was actually
worse,
or made as such,
because it forces you
out of touch
with reality
which is actually
the truth
that it can be okay
or at least get there again
BROKEN HEARTS MEND
and you get to ask
for forgiveness
and to be resisted
or maybe to be listened to
because your mistake
is not as important
as them missing you
and you've followed
the bad advice
that came from a bad place
that you were listening to
but you'll find it
more often than not
that people understand,
because the same thing
that got you in that trouble,
gets them too...
and they probably

don't know what to do,
they're just waiting
on you...
TO FORGIVE YOURSELF,
to let it go.

Know-It-All

The poet has
all the answers
his audience
gets a chance to
see if they work
he just lurks
somewhere in between
hypothesis and metaphor
ready for being ignored
or seen
as a hypothetical abstract
thing
a conjured belief
a means
to a free-spirited irresponsibility,
a dream
an example of ones refusal
to subject
to submit
who brings with him
a peace
pieced in puzzle-like formation
fitting in open spaces
and broken places
like
hearts that get their only beat
from his depart
eyes that get their only light
from his spark
fingers that get their only feeling

from his touch
and such is his dilemma
never being able
to enter
into
any symbol or resemblance
of what he meant
when he tells them to live
beyond having to commit
beyond any limit
or fragments that are figments
of an observers imagination
thinking that he
is somehow escaping
by being displaced
from normal
routines
or regulations
or his reputation
than being another
or anything other
than
stage presence
his answers bring question
and doubts
to his character
not to whether he is right
but of his right
to narrate
the plight
of the prisoners
that squander their freedom

THESE WORDS WORK.

on open-mics
and express their grievances
with likes
The poet has all the answers
and he dances
whilst no music plays
to the beat of his own drum
against the hokum
and conundrum
that the soul churns
that burn flagrantly
emitting the fragrance
of flavored trees
that waver breeze
winds blown to savor
memories
that flee
vacant scenes
of glee
that he seethes
silently
keeping to himself
the remedy
for an affliction
that injures
so many
the cure is his answers
poetry
his chance
to change
perceptions
and ways

the way he set out to
by being himself
even if it hurts
not to
be able to ask any questions
like those asked of himself
by those that pretend
to know
how
he exists.

Multiplicity

What's wrong
with saying I love you
more than once
to more than one
and meaning it
believing it
because it's true
caring
about her
and you
and you
and you
and you
fulfilling promises,
honestly
modestly arranging strangely articulate phrases that match just as
many days as it took for me to realize that I don't have desire nor the
time to spend on stopping or standing in one place long enough for
commitment to make enough sense for me to consider it outside of
whatever it represents in terms of this,
I'm faithful to who I am,
that's it
but I love you
and yes I want the best and it is not just a suggestion that I offered to
step aside so that you could find Mr.(s) "Willing to do what I won't"...
but if he is willing to give you 79 degrees and sunny, I won't,
stand in your way,
stand in your rain,
stand for your moments of now,
stand for your games

I won't,
stay
but call me
when you're imprisoned
when you need someone
to listen to you, someone to get into a debate
about faith
about waiting on mates
about haste
about the taste of your taste
about face,
don't change,
stay
because I love you
whether I'm here
or you're there
whether you care to
believe me or not
you have a choice
and this is not
pressure
this is the lesser of equals that sounds evil but is greater than or equal
to meeting you outside the box of what you speak, previously, this is
you meeting me where you dream, this is something eventually
turning into peace, of mind, one time, at a time
but repeated,
as frequently as need be,
considering someone else's
feelings,
like her
and her
and her

THESE WORDS WORK.

and maybe hers,
not mine
but being able to still love you,
the whole time...

Ignorant

We immortalize unimportant things
and remember the forgotten
like tragedy
and make people unfairly popular
blasphemy
strange fruits still hang from trees
we make diets of living things
unsuitable consumption
vomit history
long for the priceless
throughout
and trust masters
brethren despised for class
the masked just
alas
perfect words for imperfect worlds
doubt
sexual beings being ripped apart
at the seams
seemingly dissatisfied
despite bigger
dreams
biased bigots bitch about
being
without
hatred
and reality scripted
screams aloud
painted
we laugh at people

THESE WORDS WORK.

who can not help what is laughed about
definition
of evil
sacred
mistake prone perfection
lessens the expectation
responsible
safety
until it is okay
to be
human
and all the while,
We immortalize unimportant things
and remember what we should forget
like tragedy
and make people unfairly popular
blasphemy
strange fruits still hang from trees

On top.

I believe in me
I've faith I'll be
I'll make it mean,
everything
I won't just try
I'll more than survive
I will certainly thrive,
deliberately
I'll take my hits
and I won't forget
I'll suffer it surely,
courage or consequence
I'll get my due
persevered and pursued
I'll remain to it true,
intentionally
and when I success
the truth will suggest
that I was not just one,
but one of the best.

Eventually.

I will
give into you
until
I am strong enough
to fight
for myself.

The give

I wrote poems for prisoners
that were much freer than I
considered it my business
to question freedoms ire
left open interpretation
sought a song to bye and bye
gave an old bum knowledge
he'd much rather have my time
and I've thrown away poems
that should have met your ear
instead I hid them safely
beneath a whispers drear
should have spoke in turn
gave aloud the thoughts I had
but an old bums' wisdom
turned my happy sad

Dreaming dream

A
dream is
the responsibility
of mature imagination
that test possibility
with faith
and role plays
in greatness
and hides
from "safe"
in order to chase
the reality
of patience
versus
wait
and protects
what is perfect,
the energy
that procrastination
wastes
while it tries
with all its might
to stay
awake

Outside within

God
hides in the corners
of hardened hearts
in silence
cold and dark
without the blankets
of cast shadows
and doubt
that usually
keep Him warm
and His presence
out
in the open
of the land
that He created
but far too often destroyed
by His creation
that ignores
that He alone
made it
possible
to debate Him
God
cries weeping whines of worry
lines flurried
by the hatred
of impatience
with His placement
of faces
or orientation

THESE WORDS WORK.

as if
somehow
He as God
is capable
of mistakes
or waiting
for His creation
to face
His arrangement
God
is firm
on His Grace,
His patience
as He awaits
displacement
from this hate
so He waits
in the recess
of playing people
who find
or have found
evil
more accommodating
to their faith
while they believe
that God
keeps such these mercies
in His safe-
keeping
with the chase
of keeping
love,

Agape
or in a way
that allows
for fate,
His acceptance
and willingness
to say
that because of free will
it is okay.

Alcoholic

My old man withered
hidden in wrinkles
that wrote his wrongs
cans and bottles were his voice
liquor was his song
and my old man saaaang baby
years he learned the liquid notes
joined choirs and sang solos
usually sang in darkness
he hummed alone the most
knew songs from different places
shared melodies in bars
rode a bike for most my life
because he liked to sing in cars
memorized the symphonies
the aromatic sound of chord
my old man was a conductor
earned well was such reward
he saaaang, sweet and low
he saaaang, bitter high
he saaaang, comin' and goin'
he saaaang until he died
And so my old man withered
those songs sang him away
left me without those memories
and I don't wanna sang.

Mistakes

"One day"
he says
and thirty years pass
he forgets
regrets
not being able
to not be scared
to say
"I'm sorry"
for a mistake
he made
that was like other mistakes
that anyone could make
but
he can't
or didn't
see it that way
at the time
nor after
as he was running
to evade capture
by the guilt
of letting people down
and breaking someone's heart
in a moment
of weakness
and thought
thinking
way too much
about

THESE WORDS WORK.

being perfect
for once
and now
so many years later
and so easily forgotten
are the reasons
why
he did it
in the first place
and the worst case scenario
is his reality
when actually
the people he hurt
are waiting
for him
to forgive
himself
so that they can tell him
how much it hurt them
that he left

Fix

She stands
corrected
neglected to consider
herself
bitter towards rejection
so she lets
him
help
reassure her
self-
esteem
dreams of finding out
what it means
to know
rather than believe
that she doesn't need
his vision for her
to dream
or his abuse
to succeed
so she breathes
quietly
tiptoeing around his needs
to question her loyalty
or answer her inquiry
as she asks
if she's free
or if
she is just
his need

THESE WORDS WORK.

to be man enough
for the both of them
so she breathes
silently
allowing him to sleep
while she delivers
deliberately
the thing
that he needs,
manhood
she is more of the man
than her man
could ever be
but because of her pride
she lets him
lead
them
along
unequally
She stands
corrected
let it happen
again
found out who she was
through a man
no idea
of her identity
no plan
gave herself
no chance
to be
just happy

that she is
finally
free
even if
just so happens
to be
temporarily...

Prayer for Success

That this morning I awake
to meet a new embrace
that opportunity's sun
would surely touch my face
and open up my eyes
to reveal a brand new day
That upon my touch of ground
I am filled unto the brim
with an exuberance of energy
through each and every limb
to engage into the day
with accomplishment until end
That as I enter into my plans
and meet surely my ideas
I am blessed to find progression
through learning and experience
new friendship and acquaintance
with courage and commitment
That while I work to fulfill
my obligation and my dreams
I am fortunate to cherish
an abundance of such things
wishes granted at my command
and my happiness in peace
That I build reputation of faith
and a legacy of strength
as my heirs are endowed of much
from my talents and my gifts
to give forward from my bounty
as my territory is enriched

That my hands continue building
and my feet continue forth
as my mind continues thinking
and I value all it's worth
that I understand creation
that I continue such its birth
That I learn as much as possible
and I teach as much I learn
that the fire of enthusiasm
continues as I earn
for the sake of burning limits
as season takes its turn
That I find my truest passion
and with content pursue the plan
that I am disciplined in effort
to do all that I can
with a thankful mind and motion
with a grateful heart and hand
That I know for sure the reason
that I was meant to be
that I am humbled
that I believe in
my Gods success for me...

The truth

Love is
the reason
that I have no reason
to be
anything other
than myself
with you

Hidden

I've seen you
watching me
hidden
thinking that you had
ridden yourself
of my dream
for us
for the happily ever after
that we had
once upon a time
that was a treasure
that we lost
when we found ourselves
chasing
expectations
in our minds
and trying
to live
up to
the imaginations
of things
best left behind
but hidden,
in the way
of what we could have
had
had we not cared so much
about
what we thought
wasn't there

THESE WORDS WORK.

or bad
for having had known
better
than
what was in our way
those hidden things
we never found
good enough
to say

Intent

I meant to love you
meant to want you
more than I was home
or less than I was gone
show it like you desired
or somehow should have known
that I had better intentions
and that I mentioned you
didn't just distance myself
but that I had intended to
have feelings
and deal with my issues
so that I could
deal with you
I wanted to know better
so that I could help us
make it pass the rough patches
and through what kept us
from keeping promises
to be honest
about what we really wanted
no matter how it daunted
hopes and dreams
of seeing things
differently
I said that I would try
and care
less about myself
and help you to suggest
more ways for me

THESE WORDS WORK.

to relinquish
pride
and selfishness
unequally
but
with intent
hellbent
on trying
to get this
right
for the next time.

Served

Allegiance and pledge
wedged in between
commitment and service
as such with purpose
blind faith
new and nervous
tests of wills
and skills
beyond extraordinary
but ordinary
thrills of travel
that unravel inhibition
and grant wishes of farewells
and stairwells
that lead to careers
and jeers
and peers unrivaled
modes switched
from such to survival
techniques and tactics
that are acted out
in and on battlefields
and war zones
and back at home
where newscasts mean more
than updates
but sweepstakes
the winner,
who survived the day
to cheat death

THESE WORDS WORK.

and save lives
at the same time
in foreign lands
over and beyond borders
that don't welcome democracy
as moderated by visitors
or the hypocrisy
that is seen
or seems to be
the premise for invasion
of right
or what is
or the civil liberties
for what gives
sacrifice its validity
malignant gestures that jester
claims
of who is free
or brave
or enslaved
truly
civic duty
is what usually
happens
as a result of capture
salute
those who stand in the boots
firm in manning the responsibility
in response to humility
truth
honor and respects due
to whom much has been

required
veterans and troops
who prove
that freedom is dependent
upon
he or she
willing to walk through fire
for the sake
of extinguishing threats
and less credible intelligence
for the safety
security
and significance
and relevance
of an innocent resident
so residue and shrapnel
par for the course
or what happens
in war
Honor
the memory
of lives lost
cost overpaid
yet still billed
killed in lines of duty
and roadside
and strike
and for the sake
of belief
that we alike
are for peace
of some idea

THESE WORDS WORK.

that keeps us safe
here
that prevents us from
having to fear
the terroristic threats
of religions made clear
to blur the faith
of those who believe
that it is better to die
for principal
than to teach
lessons learned hard
that our hope
is breached,
wedged in between
commitment and service
In memory
and mentioning
of Stars and Stripes
stars
striped with the medals
and badges
and welts of war
and more
who we welcome home
to endure
the freedom
they fight
and fought
for.

Fall

the fall
brings with it
colors
that sing
from the voices
of leaves
that cry freedom
as they leap
to the beauty
of
this new season
for
no other reason
than that God
has
given
as a reminder
for us
to remember
to change...

Lovesense

What do you know about love
that makes it easier
that makes it reasonable
that makes it feasible
that makes it worth falling
that makes it worth calling
that makes it make sense
that makes it worth it
that makes it make you feel
like something different
something real...
Absolutely nothing.

Action

If we are to
survive
then we
must make custom
of adjustments
thrive
in substance
thrust
into function
lust
after the gumption
to do
something

Her idea...

she wants
to say I'm wrong,
I let her
she needs
a whole lot of correction before she becomes
Coretta
bet her momma
didn't tell her that
tell her facts
instead of history
mistakes did the talking
instead of the listening
say I'm not reputable
she don't know any difference
between accurate
and credible
their different
like me
and the other man
she mentions
my name to
manipulation
or masturbation
are the same two
too
to
someone who knows
better
and won't let her take
advantage

of the situation
that she enjoys
seemingly
in conversations
about why she is
or isn't
waiting
to develop,
premature ejaculation
can get you just as pregnant
but desperate
no respite
from wretchedness
no escape
or excuse
for estrogen
she wants me to be
Martin
the urban myth
the spectacle
the gift
but she has no idea
what Coretta had to deal with
greatness has an appetite
and great is the tolerance
that she
must be
filled with
despite proclivities
or realness
what I'm full of
is

THESE WORDS WORK.

real shit
extravagant means
but still thrift
accommodating the fantasy
that she has
lived with
she wants us
to be
happy
even if it so happens
that we have to make it
versus
letting nature
take its chance
I call it role play
she calls it romance

Perceived threat

She asks,
"how
can he be a man
to someone else
but
a monster to me"
I tell her
"not everyone
imagines
the monsters
you see"...

-

Posts

Sometimes
it is hard-er
to press the like button
than it is
to feel
smart-er
than the thought
of being able to do
what was posted
and then
I have to consider
the source
then force myself
to not realize
that what you uploaded
is not
what you've been down for
mostly
just words, and quotes,
loaded
hopes
and not your experience
meant to
make me feel
some type of way
or guilt
just a host
for your outer body
experience
but not necessarily

your experience
and the reason
it seems
as if you're talking about me
is the same reason
that horoscopes tend
to be true
or talking about you
because,
even broken clocks
are right twice a day
and sure as for certain
when the time is right
they will have something
to say
about
having the right
time
and so your words
are fine
it's just hard
to press comment
and say something nice
like
you should
take your own
advice
follow your own dream,
sacrifice
share in the responsibility
of the price
that must be paid

THESE WORDS WORK.

to say
things that require
cost
and the problem is
not the words you've found
but the loss
of "did as I did"
as opposed to
"did as I said"
and it is what it is
but
that is
not what I read
it is difficult
to pretend
that we are friends
but just a button press away
from being hidden
blocked and removed
because we don't agree
or because
you know
that I know
that you are
no more important
than me.

Double entendre

Poets fighting*
about poetry
about knowing things
about going about it
differently
about God
and His intent for peace
poets fighting* about
what they think
to themselves,
openly
poets fighting* about
rights and freedoms
speech and religion
evils and the system
poets fight*
they don't listen
poets fighting* about feelings
and emotions
and being hopeless
in between quotients
about potions,
potent
that are elixirs,
spoken
poets fighting* about
the politics of fights*
holograms
and sights
nights spent excited

THESE WORDS WORK.

about lights,
ideas and I did's
life
poets fighting*
about
about's
bouts with outs
and shouts
for clouts
doubts
that spout
from mouths
that pout
poets fighting* about
principles
learned from principals
put into action
by institutes
and performed
but
not listened to,
always
poets
fighting*
the fight*
for poetry
and other things
that make sense
to them
but not
to me
so instead

of fighting*
I do the opposite
and
let them be...
*insert writing/writes/write for alternate meaning

Our clothes

I remember
making stonewashed jeans
with bleach
learning hard the lessons
that momma tried to teach
and getting hand me downs
trying to turn them around
into something
neat
creases make old clothes
seem less old
wrinkled new clothes
are just bold
but I remember being told
"Doesn't matter what you wear"
"Doesn't matter that they stare"
"You just wear what I can afford"
There
I remember
wanting a "First Down"
and being told
to go out
and make some first downs
then I could have
whatever coat
that I could afford
to cover up
who I really was
and so I got whichever coat
came on

"a single mother
with three kids
and all the other bullshit that
she had to deal with"
budget
so the one
with the matching
hat, scarf, and mitts
it is
I remember
dreaming of a pair of Jordan's
knowing
we couldn't afford them
not even the thought
was economical,
my image,
comical
momma chose to be smart
because of these shoes
pros have wings
and Payless
has pro wings
momma knows best
but momma
don't know things
like the difference
between what pros wear
and those things
I remember
knowing what it was like
to want
something like

THESE WORDS WORK.

a "Gordon Gartrell",
or Used, or Damage,
or Pelle Pelle
or something airbrushed,
"Jodeci" boots
always back of the class
I wanted to front
like I had it
instead
all I had was
what was most important
at the time
but not so popular
in my mind,
the ability to remember
what it was like
to not have to worry
about it

More to it

apparently
ignorance is appropriate
socially
and must be announced
vocally
like songs that seem
out of context
or out of concept
but accepted
openly
and obviously
images must be outrageous
and contagious
and "beat faces"
are not beat faces
but cover ups
for beat faces
somehow
it's smarter to be dumb
and not just playing
numb
to the pain
of having to feel
the same hurt
over
and again
according to them
it is better to be them
than you
unless you are strong enough

THESE WORDS WORK.

to be you
in order to become
one of them
so that they
can steal your identity
and become you,
"friends"
specifically
anonymity is ridiculous,
serendipitous
but meticulously orchestrated
intuition
compared to science
evidence that there is
something to it
to the theories
conspiracies
of something bigger
like a small group
that meet
to move it
like the mountains
in the Jesus story
truthfully
there is
more to it
but
…

What is real...

There are
reasons
for believing
in ghost
but not in men
just as
it makes sense
to pretend
that things exist
that don't
that things persist
that won't
that miracles are
coincidence
prone
to interpretation
per suggestion
or incident
and ifs
cliffs fall
to bigger monsters
and dreams
come true
for impostors
and imaginations
are seen
as
options
that are like change,
constant

THESE WORDS WORK.

but not
for lack of
being sponsored
by fears
and limits
just
as thoughts
are
gimmicks
blemishes
in the skin
of accomplishment
what is endangered
is stranger
but made popular
by the same thing
there is
no such thing
as
happenstance
in capitalism
and racism
is the biggest joke
in history
fiction
the truth is
that we are all human
just different
you can't separate
what is together
just distance
it

means nothing to say
listen
if you don't
but there are reasons
to believe
in belief
as
relief
from what is
reality
the sense
of
guilt
that is
what
happens
actually,
the real.

Scars...

Every wound that I have suffered came at a cost greater than you could ever know. These are my scars, I've paid for them, I own them, they belong to me. They tell my story, they show my past, they are proof that I made it over the mountains and through the storms and beyond the obstacles that came upon me. The noise I make now was once a silence that hid me in the corners and darknesses of my despair. The smile and laughter that accompany my joy in these moments was developed on the not so funny stages that witnessed me, at my worst, but exposed for all to see, share all that I ever was with people who never really understood. My strength, my strength, well my strength comes from a GOD that, in my weakness, made me whole. He allowed me in. He acknowledged and accepted me for everything I had and had been. He saw past it and through me until I saw inside of myself, Him.

So yes I have scars, big ones. Ugly ones. Scars with dark stories and forbidden secrets. Scars with truths that I will never be able to share outside of myself. Yet I am here. And I know who I am. And I am proud of me. Scars and all.

Independent

Will they
get for me
or
for get me
no space
to figure it out
I have to live,
now
I have to survive
how
ever
the optimist
despite
the options
develop a posture
and prosper
in spite of it
in light of
this
being
whatever
the obstacle is
me
or
what was done
to me
it is profit
lost souls
that gain worlds
hurl into

THESE WORDS WORK.

glass
walls and ceilings
feelings of nothingness
match
the next level
of vulnerability
substance
abuse
scandal
profuse
usually
leave marks...
So either they
got for you
or
they
for got you
no room
to
maneuver.

I want you...

I want you
to believe me
to believe when I say
I want you
to leave me
with your heart
and start to trust
that I will lead you
feed you from afar
the things needed to be
less apart
I want you
for everything you have to offer
and no reason other
than to love you
until you feel discovered
found,
broken,
poured down upon my shoulders
let me carry you,
over
the craters of doubt
and mountains of question
into an infinity pool of certainty
where you can rest,
in
I want you
to find purpose
in my service of others
for yourself

THESE WORDS WORK.

knowing that I can help them
with your help
and know that
I'd rather not do it all,
by myself
but
I need you
for myself
I want you,
and I am confident
that my want is consciousness
an intentional constant,
yes
so that you find comfort
in my chest,
lying there or residing where
my compass rests,
guided by my heart,
let us conquer,
next
I want you
to tell me when
to see you again
and still be surprised
when I see you then
as if you didn't expect
to see me again
I want you
to mend,
to be healed
to be abandoned no more
to be separate

to be set apart
to be my priority,
once more
to be loved
to be revered
to be cared about,
much more,
I want you
to soar...
I want you
to know more about me
every moment
and learn
and share
as we're growing
and to eventually
know that all the while
you were all and exactly
what I wanted ...

Failure is not an option.

Failure is an option,
constantly
cute to say it isn't,
obviously
because success is an ugly story
and there are gruesome details
of those who prevailed
and worry
but no one wants you
to know that part
that even
the most incredible masters
have a change of heart
and doubts
that outweigh determination
and no patience
and panic attacks
hyperventilating, damaging facts
truths that were vicious lies
and questions
about how many tries it takes
before you give up
or throw in the towel,
to cover your mistakes
and anxiety
about the time
that working hard seems to waste
when easy routes and shortcuts
get you just as much
and faster

and contrary to what they speak
easy money will last you
if you do
what you're supposed to
but they won't tell you that
and I'm not supposed to
reveal that
what
"The True Hollywood Story"
of most people they tell you about
is supposed to tell you about,
that most people
only want you to know
what they tell you about
and not that
they go home to empty houses
or filled ones with no support
or no love
nor recognition
of what they are worth
just expectations
to produce
and there is a word for what you suffer as a consequence,
abuse
Failure is an option,
an excused absence
from further mediocrity
or the madness
of philosophy
that states that
you eventually get what is yours
as long as you move forward

THESE WORDS WORK.

but the truth is
some people have to give up
long before
or suffer the consequence
of believing in something else
something other than hypothesis
there is no guarantee
that you'll earn or profit
positive to what you suggest
and investing to any extent,
even in yourself,
is still a risk
and no matter how hard you try
variables still exist
You might not make it
and faith only gets you so far
and support is circumstantial
and trust is of no regard
and there is not enough
to go around
always
and way more die trying
than live doing
Failure is an option
an all too visceral vital
in spite of affirmation
or the chasing of dreams
that are never to be realized
or deemed suitable for belief
of or from those who don't see
Failure is an option
and that is why you make it

if you do
because you made another choice
because you proved
that you wanted to
that you had in sight every notion
to go forward
according to you
and you overcame obstacles
and history
and tradition
and the blues
to create color
where there was darkness
or hardly any chance of chance
and the harder it rained paralyzing adversity,
you danced
and entered forbidden territories
and opened locked doors,
kicked down or picked
and self-medicated your wounds,
bandaged up or licked
and lost sleep
and friends
and family
and hope
and your reputation
and most of anything you had
or were
saying to yourself, YES
but hearing, "NO"!
from statistics
and business plans

THESE WORDS WORK.

and formats
and the crowd
and what for?
To find out that
failure is an option
a required one for sure
much aligned with fate or destiny
a pretentious sort of lure
a devious form, distraction
an oddly noted cure,
to fail is to excel,
for all whom should endure...
Failure is an option
juxtapose to your success
but just as much responsible
for results or such your best
so kindly perceive thus disappointment
as driving force to change
and thrust forge into failure
as anecdote for pain
And keep trying,
until you fail
and until you learn
and until you win
and until you see
that failure is an option,
but your choice is to succeed!

Fire (For You)

I, once just a flicker
an alive kept spark
just barely being noticed
in an overwhelming dark
and my flame so being
as it tapered, to and fro
movement of the instant
giving me the way to go
yet burn had I always
purposed such to be
never to extinguish
it is fire, still in me
but now have I this glow
this reason to pursue
I, now a fire brightened
the reason thus is you
a fire toward redemption
a flame to recompense
be it warmth or so as it
I burn to such convince
a room no more hidden
I have torn apart enrage
I now tower as inferno
purpose so emblazoned
burn, my fire, burn
as your elements persist
I, a fire set by love,
under control of a kiss
now for you, blaze I, on
from way of your wind

THESE WORDS WORK.

a world now to conquer
till you decide its end
I, once just a flicker
on verge of letting out
you my dear found me
and set my fire about.

Work in Progress...

I am not good enough
nor will I ever be
to love you as I imagine,
or even as I see
I am only a star
you deserve every one
I am just a moon
you deserve the sun
Long to riches and favor,
spotlight and fame,
but now just an ordinary,
a much of the same
No word that I remember
or thing that I do
is sufficient to reward
the treasure of you
But yet I am fallen
a victim of sorts
under judge of your prudence
at mercy of your court
Convicted of passion
and sentenced to plea
I will spend my time serving
to the needs of your see
A slave set to master
subservient to rule
I am a clown to your circus
for your love I am fool
Thus obey as so ordered
and fulfilled as is promised

THESE WORDS WORK.

I give to thee my nothingness
a bulb to such blossom
In a garden that you've planted
a seed and fertile dirt
watered, your love and time
I will soon be thus worth
Then will I be special
as you've seen me all along
a rose in your window
a lyric in your song
And I will never be good enough
in the great that I will with your help be
to love you to the magnitude that I imagine,
or even to the deserve as I now see.

Always love...

An always love
that was
that ever goes
and returns
burns like eternal flames
the same
through challenge
and change
as strange as it may seem
yet believed
and breathed into possibility
like leaves
on fruit trees
from a juniper breeze
teasing the arms reach
of what-if's
and might-be's
and not-quite-now's
but likely's...
An always love
that always was
exactly that
an always does
exactly match
even when things
are different-ly.

Love Me

It is not as easy
to love you
as it is
to want to
but I want to
so I'll learn it,
so I'll earn it
show that I can
on demand
present myself before you
just a man
and hope that you give me ear,
or a chance
to prove it
force me to your rules
or lose it,
the chance to choose you
as I choose me,
equally
setting aside reason opposite,
deliberately
so that you make your decision,
confidently
because you had other choices
other voices to consider,
but you listened
heard a standard in my tone,
a difference
and cheered it on
hoped that I pursued you

so you readied yourself,
for the chase,
so the case I should subdue you
and that was not easy
but you learned to
let me think I knew,
while teaching me
let me think I was strong,
while weakening me
you made me cry again
and try again,
instinctively
you gave me my fire back
while extinguishing
old flames,
and the games,
and that same routine,
you blew worth into my value,
with change
and belief
not speculation, nor assumption
but release
and so I held on tighter
let down my defenses,
became the fighter,
that you knew I could be
hands held over my eyes,
but you knew I could see
you just wanted me to try,
you knew I would be
the perfect partner
once I had pulled it together

THESE WORDS WORK.

instead of parts of
strange to stand here today
standing here to say,
that I love you
in so many ways
for so many things
but for one specifically,
teaching me
to love me.

Model

We measure beauty
as if it could ever be even
and for good reason
to protect vanity
from the haunt of her secret,
that she feels ugly
that she is more than her fading identity
and so we protect her perfect
and profess her worth the sacrifice
so that she doesn't feel dirty
but that she is always looking down
at someone
on someone
for something
and so that her perfect smile
can hide crooked words
things said to her less preferred
the doubts she reflects in placed mirrors
in bathrooms she hides from the world in
until she emerges,
the worlds ten
grace that is practiced
poise that is acted
pleasant that is actually
an act as well
until she can get back to the bathroom
and wash off her only strength
in front of her reflection
that she cannot convince
to stop crying

THESE WORDS WORK.

to stop lying
to stop trying
to commit
to being more beautiful
and more sexy
her self esteem flexing its weakness
perplexing its meekness
complex is its genius
but no one sees it
that she matters not
because it doesn't matter
when you can be looked at
for being a look that flatters
and so she eats the idea,
pray she don't get no fatter
from such a big appetite
and hunger
for being loved
for more than fair skin
and high cheeked bones
and eyes that look like rainbows
and body that fits any clothes
and pretty fingers
and toes
and hair
that if she chose or not to
would flow
lips that curve naturally
and the perfect everything else
when no one else seems to notice the reality
that all this will be gone
and she will have spent all of her life

hiding behind lies
that only she knows...
and we will continue
to measure her beauty
put her on covers,
covered
in made up things
hidden by our perceptions
of made up things
and expect her to feel pretty enough
to say nothing
about her true feelings
and how she longs for a normalcy
that only being ugly brings
and that her truth is
she'd be a lot more comfortable
without being seen
for being anything other
than what anyone else sees
she'd rather measure her beauty
by the uglier means
how she is not so perfect
but just like she
that doesn't get told so often
that the ugly girl
is all the pretty girl
ever wanted to be.

Hustle

have to make it
because a few people won't let me fail
won't let me tell myself no
tell myself GO
face adversity with a fervor
looks like success
So,
up even when down
going to deserve my benefit
because I invested everything I had
until I was empty,
watch God replenish it
starts within
won't rest until I finish it
faced with the reality
this is what I wanted,
Isn't it?
fear in limited supply
courage edition limited
one of the chosen
with audacity of the abandoned
proud to face my battles
pride stranded
wrestling angels
in the spirit of Jacob,
blessings demanded
might as well go for it,
still standing
no time to stop
just watch…

branded
handed gems and little treasures
from pirates aboard measure
rest assured
pain will be overtaken,
by pleasure
no pressure
not just for me
or for my destiny
or for anything other than belief,
but forever.

Sweet tooth

Dreams are cookies
baked in the ovens of God
mixed by the smiles of angels
carefully tailored
to suit the taste
of the cookie monsters
that we all are
often not considering
the recipe
or the request
we just want the sweetness
and desires as we suggest
no matter how good
our favorite ones are...
I like the chewy kind
and the warm ones
and the big ones
and the fresh ones,
the really good ones...
I always remember the good ones.

You love me

I love you,
Perfectly.
for loving the perfect me
the one with all the cracks,
Beautifully.
taking my breath away,
but letting me breathe
so studiously
your care and concern
tutoring me
showing me how to be a better person
while rooting for me,
I love you,
Certainly.
as sure as assured my secure is
but with the fragility of the truth
that my pure is
you give me strength,
I can endure this
so obscure was my proof at one time
that I thought I would lose it
and who but you saw me falling
and proved it
that I was safe all the while
of my choosing
using your heart as my resting place
usually
I love you,
for believing,
and leaving me no choice

THESE WORDS WORK.

but to leave
to fly away
to see
that what gives me flight
are my wings
and you are there to witness
or be the wind beneath
no matter when
or where
I decide
to be...
Because, you love me.

This me... (No one knows)

Tears run down my face
no sounds
sounds bound by fear
but I speak loud,
usually
no tears
no one knows this me
trapped insecurities
parading as belief
leaving me to believe
that no one
not one
understands me
or stands for me
or is willing to be
what I need
an example of how to
how to
be free
or just be
without the caution...
Lost in my transgression
was my transition
transferred from who I was
to this place here
position
from unknown
to unmentioned
just a speck in the I of who once ago was
a condition

THESE WORDS WORK.

a rendition of a caged birds song
a listen
a vision of remembrance,
history
No mystery that I am as I have
found myself to be loved
for things I hate about me
helpless to fix the brokenness,
an identity
the way I know myself
like in the dark,
the only place I can see
so I find myself
alone
or always trying to be,
purposely
in the company of an imagination
that always loves me
for me
and proves it,
by consistency
consistently,
destroying me
Showing me all of the things
that are wrong
about me
and how all that I wait for
had gone without me
because I was too proud
too proud to doubt me
because I wanted to feel,
authentically

wanted to be loved,
appreciatively
wanted to be aware,
instinctively...
instead I sit here
with these tears,
silently
trying to make sense,
of simple things
just wanting nothing more
than to breathe,
unrestrictedly
wanting to turn on the light
so that I am seen
wanting to fight
for the right of me
and stop the travel
of this blinding plea
this has gone on forever,
in spite of me
I had even lay across the tracks
before the train could leave
and wouldn't you know,
it was going east
so from the ground,
I watched it flee
instead of what it should have,
run over me
but what more could I've known
I've such awful luck,
faithfully
just keep on surviving,

THESE WORDS WORK.

such fateful things
and writing these stories
that no one sees
or seems
to believe
are me...
So the tears run down my face
with no sounds
the sounds bound by fear
even but I speak loud,
usually
with no tears,
yet, no one knows this me

Love, finally.

Someone wants a love
that wants them
that flaunts them
without secret
and yet private
mature
but wild yet
with no inhibition
willing to listen
that mentions how much
it can't be without
someone wants a love so sure
and with no doubt
a love that escapes fear
and foolish mistakes
a love that takes,
chances
a love willing to dance
to old songs
but with new moves
and romance
a love that stands outside
and waits
or cries
just to get your attention
enough to shift your sadness
to gladness
for enough of a while
to be the ever after
that captures the smile

THESE WORDS WORK.

that precedes the laughter
that seems to just blurt out
faster
than it did before
when it wasn't love
but instead
longing
to be released
from being free
because someone wants
to be captured
by love
Immediately...

My wish for you...

I want to see you happy.
I want to see you free.
I want to see you healthy.
I want to see you BE.
I want to see you loved.
I want to see you living.
I want to see you at peace.
I want to see you giving.
I want to see you fruitful.
I want to see you blessed.
I want to see you appreciated.
I want to see you in success.
I want to see you emotional.
I want to see you feeling safe.
I want to see you in your element.
I want to see you in your space.
I want to see you celebrated.
I want to see you being known.
I want to see you rest assured.
I want to see you on your own.
I want to see you with your family.
I want to see you purposed.
I want to see you understanding.
I want to see you serving.
I want to see you full of joy.
I want to see you wide with hope.
I want to see you chase a dream.
I want to see you find it lo.
I want to see you rested.
I want to see you strong.

THESE WORDS WORK.

I want to see you faithful.
I want to see you home.
I want to see you such a star
I want to see you shine so bright,
that I can see you in the distance,
that I can always see your light.

Rescued... (for Love)

Love has
found itself
inside of me
like white sand beaches
finding me
blinded
by the sunsets
and wet
and near the water
barefooted
and rested
with the giver of things
comfort
and dreams
naked
inspired by the feeling
kneeling in the soul
peeling off the layers
of the old
freed
to be bold
silent sensation
speaking louder
than conversations
that hold the promise
of being honest
with myself
afforded the luxury
of being
on my own

THESE WORDS WORK.

with someone else
for no other reason
than is that
I can
have the pleasure
of being measured
a treasure,
myself
and backed by a gold
that values me whole
a soul rescued
by someone else...
the idea more tangible
than ever
that there is
something better
than a loneliness
that once kept me,
forever
thank you,
white sand
and ocean
beautiful breeze
and the notion
that a view is worth the loss
of not ever seeing the cost
that was paid
to bring me
closer
to you
that day...

Regrets... (of Love)

Sometimes the words
we never think to say
are the ones that hold the power
to give us the strength
to do what we never would
because we don't ever think
we ever could feel the type of way
that we do about the things
that seem to go away
before we ever get the chance to say
that we'd love to have them stay...
and comes a night like this
when want is such a kiss
a touch upon the lips
of a something so I miss

Don't be so hard on YOU.

Don't be so hard on yourself!
Today's lenders, yesterday's borrowers
This mornings leaders, yesterday's followers
Those who judge and legislate now,
surely fell certain to mistake once ago
Those who teach and profess in the present
once surely did not know
He that is expert in such field of expertise
that was him that came as novice
'Till he learned and grew and learned so more
a now success was then a promise
A "greatest" mother was just once a daughter
A doting father, just a rebellious son
Had failure not been a certain option,
neither victories could have been won
A realized dream was a crazy thought
a best friendship, once bickering foes
A depth not measured by the mountainous highs,
instead characterized by torturous lows
The rich we're once poor
the haves, not always so
solutions used to be problems
stop, became of go
So stop, my child, and play
learn brilliance from your bruising
give time a chance to welcome you
let experiment be of your choosing
Feel first the fire of temptation
let rage the rain of your will
quit not because of any limitation

remember that life is yet life, still...
and remember...
Today's lenders where yesterday's borrowers
This morning's leaders, yesterday's followers!

Abandoned, reckless.

You left some words behind...
forever, always, and until
you walked out of the door with them on the table,
next to some pills
a glass filled with what looks like water
guess I'm supposed to chase them
with what I discover is a container of your tears,
I know, because I taste them
you left some thoughts on the bed,
I found your feelings on the floor,
you left your emotions in the closet,
I found your pride behind the door
your stare is still at the window,
your hope is down the drain,
I just tripped on your ego in the bathroom,
I found a pillow still warm with your pain
You left an angry message on the mirror
I decoded it with mist
as I stood alone in our shower
trying to picture this
your despair is still on the couch
your ambition still in the drawer
I just noticed your keys on the wall
what are you walking for?
You left some words behind...
I'm sorry, forgive me, let's try
maybe you forgot them in your rush,
maybe you'll get them next time.

Relentlessly

Relentlessly
missing you
thoughts of some chump kissing you
pissing me off,
but I burnt that bridge
and now we live on either sides,
worlds apart,
you over there with him,
me over here, with your heart
wishing you'd come back to get it
I've hidden it next to my feelings
the ones I pretended not to have
well I'm ready to give them to you now
public displays, passwords, and poetry
not just my emotion, but my most important things
whatever it takes
just to have you fall asleep next to me
I don't know what else to say,
PLEASE
The truth is that you'll never trust me again
the way I need you to
you'll always have a doubt in your mind
and a reason too
so you'll love me with caution
halfway, all or, something,
somewhere in between everything I'm asking for,
and nothing
but I deserve it
every way you could have possibly been hurt,
I learned it

THESE WORDS WORK.

and had the nerve to graduate into master
what I did to you seemed like a joke
what you're doing to me now seems like laughter
but I deserve it
finally standing up for myself,
nervous,
down on my knees,
PLEASE
we met under different circumstances
signs, wonders, and predictions
chances
an entire universe ahead of us,
understand-ed
and here we meet again
as if the plan was
to still feel the same way
how could we have grown so far apart
and still feel the same way
how could I see you after all this time
and feel the same way
as if everything and everyone else happened,
to make us more suitable
I still see you the way I've seen you every second since,
beautiful
like a John Legend verse
under an acoustic sky
on a day like today
in arms like, mine
beautiful,
PLEASE
allow me to steal pictures
and glimpses,

they'll have to make due for kisses
I'll keep saying that I'm fine with us being over
that'll make due for how much I miss you,
emails and random anonymous phone calls,
those will make due for distance,
PLEASE
in the meantime,
just say that I'm not hurting alone
say that you wish things were different,
say that you'll reconsider tomorrow
say that you've moved on, reluctantly
but say that you held on as long as you could,
hoping for me
say that you remember something about us
that he can never do
say that you know that I'll meet someone else
but no one ever like you
say that you'll remember me forever
say that you'll save a place in heaven for me
say that I can still feel this way about you,
no matter what
and you don't even have to say,
PLEASE.

Speak my mind....

We love
to love
dangerously
In the company of anticipation,
impatiently
saying things like,
wait for me
A flicker now a flame,
that became
burning towards one another
the same
embers that destroy
any attempt to flee
no one ignites you,
like me,
says she
Long pauses
and withdrawal
longings
and belongings
strewn about our past
Yet,
they last
Inadvertent opinions
assumptions
by the plenty,
thoughts and dreams
that seem so real
for the way they feel
And still no one

to replace
the pain
nor the pleasure
no one has found
your trouble
or your treasure
like me,
says she
Mistakes
evolved
escaped into
misunderstandings
that enthralled
our curiosity
to believe
that we
were either
meant
or
to be
but definitely
a measure,
in between
A clarity,
one of us a drug
the other of us,
a fiend
a jones about this fix,
intermittently
but hooked,
nonetheless
on such this thing

THESE WORDS WORK.

and it's obvious
like she says,
we can't fight this,
this is need
So we play distance
like its free
meanwhile
paying a cost,
Everything
to be
the one
that got away,
like me.

Decidedly

without you
I still find ways
to make it
about you
days
that drag along
since we've seen
one another
seem so long
and far apart
but I find myself
easily
thinking
about
how much I remember
and your heart
the way you
opened it up for me
to start
and how I make a mess
every time
the darkest days
behind us
my troubled ways
only there to remind me
of the sighs
that accompany
the silence
that sneaks upon us
in between
the heavy breathing
when I'm leaving
with no return date
but you wait
every time
a promise

THESE WORDS WORK.

to do nothing more
than change
for the better
and
not find myself
somewhere else
for whatever
especially not
for something better
when I could have
done that a long time ago
or never
but you let me
explain
every time
a conclusion
that I've come to
is that
I know
what I want
and you have
no reason
to leave me
because
I'm worth being
believed in...
Every time.

Write for You...

I want to write for you
play the sound of these words
loud and verbatim,
until you hate them
until you make them memory
and remember me
I want to write for you
a serenading sound that rhymes
and lies to you vividly
like feel good music
on bad days
and a melody
that helps you escape,
the misery
I want to write for you
personal touches
and subtle nuances
untold secrets
and hurt that do unto others
like only music can do
give me your attention,
I want to write for you
I want to write for you
arrange a great array of piece
compose a concerto
and speak
through my instrument
wet your palette
for my music
so that you choose it,

THESE WORDS WORK.

instantly
I want to write for you,
mentally
I want to write for you
I want to write for you
bass lines
and strings
percussions that bring life
and verbiage that means
nothing
until you are near it
I've written a song for you,
come hear it
A song about that first night
of passing by
me wanting your attention
you asking why
and how we played
like a back and forth sonnet,
a deceptive honesty
a tragic romance,
comically
as we frolicked over both,
snares and stares
an audience of our own being,
shared
I wrote a song about it...
an instrumental,
coincidentally
a rhythm awaiting your tune,
lyrically
a theme song,

for our motion picture,
Come sing it with me,
the words that I write for you
in chorus
and harmony
for us,
to the sound of free
muted for no reason,
but to savor the sound
of a better noise,
our heartbeats
dancing against the tempo
of our bodies,
especially,
When we sing.

It Blows... (Death)

There will be a wind that blows
it will carry on your words
it will throw to and fro the tide,
it will uplift the birds
A wind that flies over my face
and carries about some leaves
a wind that bends apart clouds
a wind going about the trees
A wind that flies a child's kite
and cools a sunny day
a wind that closes shut a door
a wind that causes one to sway
There will be a wind that howls
there will be a wind that squeals
there will be a wind that hurts
there will be a wind that heals
A wind that grows the flowers
a wind that spreads so life
there was a wind this morning
there is a different wind tonight
For now upon the wind
I must capture what is gone
a wind we once shared together
has carried you along
So now these winds remind me
these winds must let me know
that you are now a wind
as I must let you go...

Our Father, or not...

Daddy...
Because not every intention
turns into action
and sometimes a mess
remains a mess,
quite matter-of-factly
Expectations
don't always translate to great
hope might often be hurt
need will sometimes be late,
or never at all
and "supposed to had" risen,
might fall
A responsibility
can be abandoned
and a role can fall short
what some might treat as game,
some perceive sport
for one, be it rule
for another, be it fool
for both, be it court
Unheralded accomplishment
purpose versus pressure
either way of roads traveled
lead to journeyed lesson
Love is an uneven trade
a bar greased and left to bare
only the prepared shall survive
and even them,
sometimes unfair

THESE WORDS WORK.

food on a table
a check in the mail
an attendance on the sideline
a balance of the scales
or not
Or a reason why
or not
Or a try
or not
Bad examples lead
to better stories
and become motivation
for a beaming glory
just like hurt feelings
become kept promises
and well told lies
become traits of honesty
and probable, becomes probably
History teaches
that no man is perfect
but a chance towards perfection
makes investing in every little boy worth it
because he might grow to be different
than what fate considered deserving
and he might do differently
what was his only way of learning
and he will leave no slack in the line
but that needed to bait
and he will carry into his wellspring
the full bounty of grace
and a mothers pillow will
only soak in tears of self

would be a perfect dream
if wished upon itself
but things often change
than what we did perceive
so mother may have to mother
more than she once believed
or not
Because maybe daddy will stay
or not
Or maybe just explain
or not
Or maybe just refrain
from being Daddy
or not
and thus quite the opposite
can be motive for accomplishment
And so steps can be taken
and steps made
and steps can become titles
and steps laid
and steps can lead the way
from bad days
... stepdad can serve
just as well,
and sometimes much better
the past says
Because...
Ugly ties
and macaroni plaques
are no selector of persons
they come with the respect
so long as the mentor

is no meant to be
then brothers
and uncles,
all men can be the fathers
eventually
Or not
and instead
an image or an inspiration
will drive forward the cause
and God will be our Father,
a just Father to us all...

Self-Imploded

Truth is that
the soundtrack that he lived by,
killed him
filled him with an ambitious idea,
thrilled him
opened him up to that life,
sealed him...
Same song
that the drive by'er drove by to,
is the same song,
his friends cry to
see him as just another reason
to not believe any different
because the truth is this:
you might die too,
whether or not you try to
niggaz gon' kill niggaz
that's just what niggaz do
problem is we ain't niggaz,
that's why we're uncomfortable
But not enough to get up
and turn the station
or the channel
or away from the images
that cause the damage
we just lie on the couch,
famished
thirsty for something else,
tired of feeding as we've been,
on nothingness

THESE WORDS WORK.

but refusing to do better,
or at least something else
So we sit and watch
or ignore
or get affected just enough
to get bored
and act like all these funerals
we can afford
to sit through
or applaud
at the end
of sermons,
or poems
that say we've had enough
of the violence
and that we've learned…
yet, that one song
is still the jam
no matter the jam it got us in
no matter that the rappers delight
is now to sin
to mislead our babies
to rape our women
and our men
of any virtue that we once beheld,
from within…
but the Bad Boy made good,
the Nigga With Attitude found his beat,
you either grind or rest,
and "Suckaz" are those who sleep…
And,
Truth is that the soundtrack that he lived by,

killed him
filled him with an ambitious idea,
thrilled him
opened him up to that life,
sealed him...
Same song
that the drive by'er drove by to,
is the same song,
his friends cry to...

What's next... (After I'm so...)

Hope the reflections bring about respect
Thinking about those back in the days
make me wonder about what's next
You for it
Or just flex?
It was bad back then, no lie
Gangs, drugs, rap music, and some guns
But we had "stop the violence" movements
we were able to move around, some fun
There was beef,
legit or not
But there was a sense of order
we had spots
There was community
and a sense of pride
but somewhere in between Harold and Hadiyah,
It died
And music went from
Common to a mindless behavior
as Jesus alternated
between a charm and a Savior,
either way Jesus ain't gone save us
We are responsible for applying the lessons that the story of Jesus gave
us
I remember when you were "bogus" or "out of pocket"
and somebody "called it" for the blocks
When you were able to post up on the porch,
a legitimate neighborhood watch
We used to kick it
whether you were "sent off" or "on a mission"

and the real D-Boys wanted to do something good
and we listened...
and I miss it
Social media has made us anti-human
propaganda got us believing the hype,
undue influence
opposition prepared post put us in the paint,
from righteous to ruin
The media, the madness, this mess,
congruent
So now we "turn up" instead of turn out
we went from "burnt up" to burnt out
and the old heads are tired
Everything they worked for,
didn't really work out
We brought into being independent
without independence
and such we scattered about our history
without any dependents
from the first descendants
to being first offender defendants
Ignorant
I remember when hustle was hard work
until you came up
That was how we came up
now the hustle is to hustle
Rob, Steal, and Kill
that's how they came up,
then call it "squad"
so they gang up
bad representation,
society blame us

THESE WORDS WORK.

Indignant
And still we skirt the real issues
fighting for freedoms in no mans land
400 years of hurt and still mis-used
Stuck in a religious time warp,
No matter what God ole mastuh gave us,
them still his views
And our inheritance
became irrelevant
It was once intelligence
became benevolence
feasting from the rations of a welfare portion
that's not heaven-sent
So the "I'm so" is the "oke doke"
a nice distraction for the brunt of jokes
and debating legislating plants
is the blunt of smoke
We still got probationary voting rights
Evil is evil, you can't vote it right
the miseducation taxed Lauryn Hill
and making niggaz laugh axed Dave Chappelle
what story shall we tell?...
Too many babies, too many babies
burying children, too many lately
Too many ways to explain it off
who do we blame, it's OUR own fault,
We brought into it, WE brought them to it
WE have to call it off!
So,
I hope these reflections bring about respect
the good ole days are gone,
What's next?

Mission "Aborted"

My city is known
for abortions
of Black Youth,
they might tell you different
but I got proof:
at least 21 attempted this weekend,
at least 3 went through
no medical card needed,
any age is approved
How are we Blaming Chief Keef
for "Indian in our family" problems
Mayor pass on responsibility,
Folks say Hoover can solve 'em
but this ain't nothing new,
It's a blood renaissance,
no Harlem
Chief say it's a gun issue
but that's not accurate
We can find the guns
Where are the advocates?
While we ignore the 70 story elephant
the propaganda is evidence
but that's not relevant...
This ain't about races,
It's about location
We call it Chi-Raq,
They want their city back,
they're impatient
They redlined the red-liners

THESE WORDS WORK.

until they had secured enough tax dollars and subsidies to grant reason and justification to plead for their safety,
Lately...
They've been building up barriers and buying back Bronzeville, putting off projects to refurbish the projects, while pushing the problem further south,
Meanwhile,
The wild hundreds doubled,
our decimals subtracted
we aren't supposed to remember
so we reacted...
According to plan
And meanwhile,
schools close
like soup kitchen doors
after dinner
as if hunger only takes place
between the hours they give us,
BUT,
watch what they do
with those buildings
Non-talk of the real issues
while these kids walk
in these still issued,
no matter how they help you play,
they still gym shoes
Nike made 2 billion bucks,
gave Jordan a house nigga cut,
But...
We got dem J's tho
and can play some spades Bro
Rap used to be different,

CORNELIOUS "SEE" FLOWERS

I remember them days, Yo!
But,
They deliver abortions here
on-site services
any age group is eligible
for no reason purposes.

I like you, plain...

Without every detail
no explanation needed
You're here in my presence,
you've succeeded
I don't care about your past
you're human just like me
we've both made mistakes
we can call it history
No need to defend your attitude
I know how to calm it down
I'll let you be yourself
I know you'll come around
I like you plain
The way you laugh
The way you cry
The way you react to my antics
The way you try
Make up sex with familiar moves
No need to act like you haven't
I already know that you do,
and I'm cool
My baby used to be his baby,
she my baby now
don't bother me a bit,
she my baby now
Let out your insecurities
pick up your low self-esteem
give me a chance to acknowledge you
and I won't ever let you leave
Because I like you plain

Whichever way you feel comfortable
is up to you
I want it,
I want to,
I want you...
So,
Whether you want a penthouse
or a picnic,
I'm getting it
Low-rise jeans
or high rise means,
we can fit in it
Cocoa butter or Mac
you'll get no flack from me
nose in the air pretty
or "hand me my Vaseline" ready
you are all right with me
I like you plain
T-shirts and sweats
don't forget the sneakers
court side or in the box,
but you don't forget the bleachers,
So when the time comes for success
you let failure teach us
how to appreciate the features
and still remain the same...
Because you like it plain
No gimmicks or getting over,
we're getting older
no time to improvise real love
we're getting bolder
So we can face ourselves

THESE WORDS WORK.

religiously
In the spirit
continuously
bringing forth the gifts of being,
beautifully stated,
I wanted plain
so I waited…
Made it through trends and fad
hot, cold, nice, and bad
things I thought I'd never do
and words I would never use
Her's, She's, the one's,
and the "I don't know why's",
All to get to you…
To put it plainly,
You remain a constant variable
a certain and consistent love
whether I'm missing
or maturing to marry you
while you decide if I'm worth it,
all the mess you've tarried through…
The reasons, The seasons
the things that I believe in
dumbed-down or genius
my appearances, then leaving
vanishing acts, my steady
the eagerness, the not-so ready
that levy that broke
and flooded into your city
you took me in
you took pity
yet not enough to enable

so you stabled me
taught me the manners of love,
tabled me
Old-fashioned way,
and change...
I like you, plain.

Don't Shoot.

Don't shoot...
down his dreams
before he begins to believe
before he begins to see
before he leaves
He's unarmed
unharmed by expectations
undaunted by limitations
unwavering,
just waiting
Give him space,
he's pacing
Tired from chasing down doubts
constant accusation
and outs
no amount of assurance
no insurance
just endurance
He is a purist
Please don't shoot
Little black boys have become target practice
their mothers forced to become activists
absentee fathers become advocates
or inactive
while the police laud them all
with laughter,
it's fashion
Cell phone camera's scream "ACTION"
but these ain't actors
Its the music

Its the attitude
Its the sagging pants
Its the dread-locs
... But these ain't factors
He is an addict
to capitalism
and orgasm
and momma's religion
and television
So, please don't shoot
him up
through intravenous means
without making sure that he knows
what intravenous means
he's been drugged
through intravenous means
doubt
statistics
stereotypes
assumptions
conclusions
pressure
stressors
He is well acquainted with these
before he knows what any of it means
an antidote is what he needs
Please don't shoot
videos that lead him astray
says the wrong things
and music the radio play
has the wrong theme
he is confusing comedy

THESE WORDS WORK.

with abuse
but celebrity makes it right
and the only way to choose
either live that life
or lose
so they say
But that is no excuse,
Don't shoot,
Stop shooting down the competition
in attempt to abort their mission
STOP GUNNING DOWN OUR BROTHERS
because you don't want to listen
and hear their TRUE STORY
or let them discover
what you and yours did
that is why you abhor him
because he is finding out
and you are too old,
to be hiding out
can't keep up with the internet
or what him taltmbout
but why shoot?
Too many calls to 911
man down, R.I.P
and the Reason Is Police
Get it?
The reason he's deceased
In front of his procession is awareness
In the distance is disbelief
we know how to be,
"FREEZE"
and saying "PLEASE",

Don't shoot.

Name calling...

You call him KING,
You crown him
You call him NIGGA,
You down him
You call him NOTHING,
You clown him
I know,
I'm around them
Found them to be more susceptible to success at the mere suggestion
of possibility
Nothing to do with an unwillingness to comply,
but ability
They don't have an opportunity to try
Just pressure to produce
and if you are going to find a problem with him either way,
He figures, whats the use?
This poem is for those of us being lied to
For those whose intentions got lost in the intermission of life,
I know you tried to
but before you could ascend,
You were accosted or assumed to
And as soon as you do,
They bury you
without a funeral,
I've got proof
and the scars too
speaking of speaking into existence,
Stop saying you got bars fool
They got bars too!
Daddy say we dun had too many signs,

He's right, I've heard "Hell Yea" in too many rhymes,
that's the law of attraction
Repeat this 20 times...,
Loud too...
Trap music
Trap music
Trap music
Trap music
Trap music
Trap music
Trap music
Trap music
Trap music
Trap music
Trap music
Trap music
Trap music
Trap music
Trap music
Trap music
Trap music
Trap music
Trap music
Trap music
Trap music
It's that music, and music like it
that leads us wrong,
We were once a product made possible by freedom songs
unfinished business,
they beat us
then feed us wrong
got us in the paint, back to the basket
leading us on

THESE WORDS WORK.

we need to be gone
but instead we're asking the big bad wolf
to lead us home...
You call him KING,
You crown him
You call him NIGGA,
You down him
You call him NOTHING,
You clown him
I know,
I'm around them
Truth is that we got egg on our face
ran at the first sign of smoke
and yelled fire
But it was arson
scrambled his story,
you can tell he's lying
but we launched into full scale attack
and jumped on faulty bandwagons
driven by media
making insignificant issues out of locs,
and pants saggin
ass backwards
but demand action,
expedient
Oh, but that's the scam,
catch it...
They pass out strikes
like chalkboards in math class
then tell him he don't count
until he got cash
but he can't count

so he got mad
and he can't count on the system,
they got Dad
Momma counted on him
until it got bad
then she just blamed him
cause he count stash
everybody else counted him out
so he bout mad
and all he ever wanted to do was count,
matter of fact
You call him KING,
You crown him
You call him NIGGA,
You down him
You call him NOTHING,
You clown him
I know,
I'm around them
No sense in blaming Mr. White
when we complain about Mr. Right
steady playing Mr. Nice
putting it off until tomorrow
because we don't feel like explaining this, tonight
And change gon' come
been anthem since our ancestors
change gon' came and went
we just a chantin'...
(Sing with me)
Fuck bitches
Get money
Thug life

THESE WORDS WORK.

Who want it
Pop that
Shake dat
Take that
Take that
Take that
Take that...
Like you're supposed to
because of what you're exposed to
because you were told to
not because you chose to
I told you,
You call him KING,
You crown him
You call him NIGGA,
You down him
You call him NOTHING,
You clown him
I know,
I'm around them.

She fell in love, with words.

She fell in love with words
words never meant for her
words that he spoke in general
words never meant to infer
She heard him say fidelity
as he spoke of a commitment
she got lost in his translation
I wish she would have listened
She drew of a conclusion
that was never soon to be
she thought she heard her man
she thought that man was he
He was only speaking theory
and had never thought it more
she heard him tell a story
she yearned him tell her more
Just as she had prayed
just as had been promised
but she had only seen his pretty
she ignored that he was honest
She fell in love with words
head over heels in fact
she gave his words a color
and she painted him with that
A blue to mask her sadness
A red to mask her pain
A green to give her value
A brown to keep her plain
A yellow that was bright
A pink that made her feel

THESE WORDS WORK.

A white that gave her balance
A black that made her real
And soon there was a picture
inside of her museum,
she invited all to see it,
as she praised the artist, him
Counted herself as his muse
imagined what he felt
she constructed such an image
did it all and by herself
But he was none the wiser
not a clue what she had done
she was only for the moment,
He was only having fun
And there were other ones,
just like her in fact
that were as important to him,
and surely had his back
But never was he distracted
he seemed always there, sure
alone had been her sickness
she discovered him as cure
She fought to keep him present
made amends and compromise
she made need out of desire
she made love out of lies
And if it wasn't for his words,
then maybe she would see
that maybe she was wanted,
by a different man, like me.

What if...

What if you were here
to serve him
and her
and then
to praise high
fellows
and worship
in concert
the lesser
of men
and honor
of your heart
and mouth
the doctrine
of that which is,
them
What if the God
that you are to believe
breathed,
an innocent bystander
cleaved
along side of a road
that you are
all too willing
to leave
What if "Amen"
was an ode to a man
in speaking to all men
being that God was
just a man

THESE WORDS WORK.

or first a man
or-esque,
a man
And what if
none of it
that had been
of significance
been significant
or anything more
than impotent
towards making
a difference
because you found no same
in the different
and such
made no difference
while making
only progress
but no sense of it
a shame,
isn't it?
Because what if
God
was asking Himself
who himself was
because He had
somehow forgot
for no reason other
than, because
because He had
gotten distracted
with all of the other stuff

that had become
from the simple
that His intention
once was
what if
you missed the point
hitting the mark
or refused to see the light
because you were afraid
of the dark
and got left behind,
carrying the spark
what if
what mattered
was what mattered
what if
we were more aware
of the moment
and less obsessed,
with after
and in such genius
realized
that the purpose
was laughter
born of comedy
that picked fun equally,
honestly
but wasn't badgered
wasn't based in hatred
and wasn't taken
so seriously
or literally

THESE WORDS WORK.

but was instead
exactly
what was needed
to heal the sickness
of greed and envy
and so it healed
and cured
and left power
in the tombs
of old wounded bigots
and covered holes
like divots
and made truces
and compromise
the standard
what if
what if we demanded
to see justice
just as much as we seek
just is how
we bring peace
what if
what if
what if
we didn't sleep?

God-less

How is
your God
more God
than
my God
why is your God
more believable
to have faith in
and less vulnerable
to interpretation
than the God
to my liking
where is your God
while slaves
and innocents
are suffered
to ignorance
does your God forget
or remember it
when is
your God
coming
to explain him
or her
self
or at least
help
what is
your God
doing

THESE WORDS WORK.

while the devil
everyone agrees on
uncovers his stealth
is your God impressed
why does
your God
judge
but not jury
while you see unseen
is His vision blurry
while you rush to assume
why doesn't He hurry
must your God be late?
or does your God hate,
your views
just as much
as I do.

About the Author

Writer, Performer, Poet, and Author, **Cornelious "See" Flowers** is a Chicago based artist with over 25 years of action and experience in the motivational and inspirational space. Known for his amazing and awe-inspiring works, "**See**" has survived and overcome a lifetime of challenges and adversity with a strength and resilience that is magnificent to witness. Through his printed work, social media presence, live performances and speaking engagements, "**See**" has built a platform that is celebrated and acknowledged globally for his wisdom and direction.

A Husband, Father, and Community Leader, "**See**" continues to MOTIVATE, INSPIRE, and ENCOURAGE through everything that life presents, with a positive message and example for all.

For more information, booking inquiries, and other opportunities, please contact "**See**" via email @: **booking@seethepoet.com**

Read more at www.seethepoet.com.

Milton Keynes UK
Ingram Content Group UK Ltd.
UKHW042034031224
452078UK00001B/112